THIS

WAS

SEX

WHICH WILL YOU CHOOSE ?

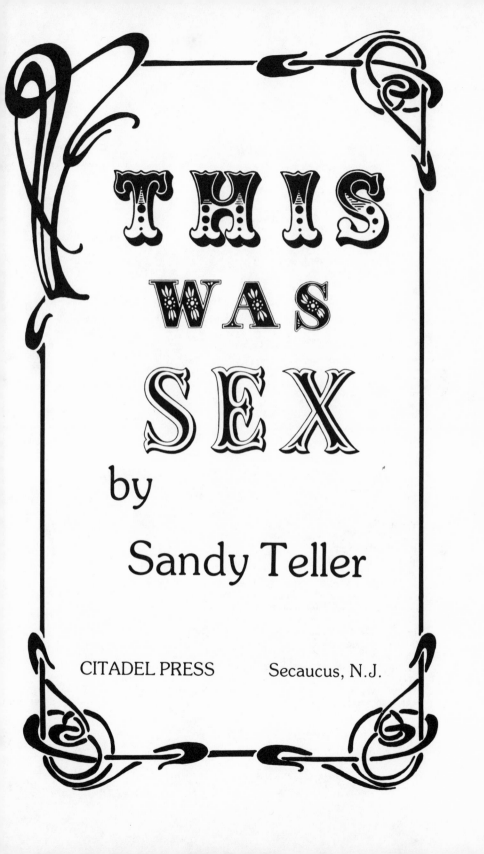

THIS WAS SEX

by

Sandy Teller

CITADEL PRESS   Secaucus, N.J.

First edition
Copyright © 1978 by Sandy Teller
All rights reserved
Published by Citadel Press
A division of Lyle Stuart Inc.
120 Enterprise Ave., Secaucus, N.J. 07094
In Canada: George J. McLeod Limited, Toronto
Manufactured in the United States of America

Library of Congress Cataloging in Publication Data
Main entry under title:
This was sex.
    1. Sex — Anecdotes, facetiae, satire, etc. 2. Sex — Addresses, essays, lectures.
I. Teller, Sandy.
PN6231.S54T48   820'.8'0353   77-25217
ISBN 0-8065-0611-3

Several years ago, on the floor of the Senate-Chamber, a distinguished Senator uttered language concerning the immoralities and crimes of the American people to which the world listened with astonishment.

A general affection of incredulity, a disposition to ridicule the speeches and anathematize the speaker, were widely used to weaken the force and to neutralize the benefits of the expose so boldly proclaimed; but the conscience of the nation had been awakened, the "ball had been set in motion."

[A Physician (Nicholas Francis Cooke), *Satan in Society*, 1876.]

DOCTOR CALLS SEX
LAUGHING MATTER

Marseilles, France — Dr. Lucienne Rosay, 52, promised newlyweds and young mothers here that "most marital problems will disappear when we see that sex is a laughing matter."

The marriage specialist said, "The contortions of the act are hilarious. It's time for joy, jokes and giggling," insisted the doctor.

"How ridiculous that so many lovers today should let it bring them misery and anguish."

[*Philadelphia Evening Bulletin*, May 12, 1977.]

A FULL AND ACCURATE DESCRIPTION OF WHAT MEN AND WOMEN DO WITH EACH OTHER (circa 1915)

"You needn't be frightened, darling. You remember what I told you. When Uncle Tom gets to thinking of Little Eva he gets very proud and stands straight up. He gets very big and — and strong, and stands erect. It's Nature makes him do that. In fact little Eva wants him to do it."

"Wants him — why wants him?"

"Well, you see, Little Eva really wants him to come and play in her garden, and the only way for him to get in the gate is to carry himself very stiff and strong. I didn't finish the fairy story the other day. You remember when I — when I played with Little Eva like this" — he placed his hand between her thighs and she gave a convulsive start at the caress — "you felt a wonderful sensation, didn't you?"

"Yes — yes," she murmured.

"Well, that is the kind of sensation you will feel when Uncle Tom at last is admitted to the garden and allowed to play there. Only it will be much more wonderful.

"There is no other sensation like it — no other delight that mortals can experience anything like so delectable as this. And the same supreme pleasure comes to Uncle Tom as well.

"After he has been playing in the garden awhile he gets very excited, they both get tremendously excited.

"But that isn't all.

"Uncle Tom is a sort of gardener in his way and always carries seed around with him. When he gets into Little Eva's garden, he gets ready to sow the seed. He never sows it until he gets excited enough, but when the climax of his joy and excitement comes, he sows the seed. Then it almost seems as if his mission was ended.

"As soon as he has sown his seed he knows his visit is over. He says goodbye to Little Eva and comes out as meek as you please.

"He goes into her garden full of pride and importance, big and stiff and strong, and when he has done his duty and sown his seed, he becomes so small and limp you would hardly think he was the same Uncle Tom.

"Do you think you understand all this, sweetheart?"

She sighed. "I understand it a great deal better than I did. You make it sound rather romantic and — nice, somehow."

[Anonymous, *The Honeymoon.*]

CONTENTS

This book is respectfully dedicated to men, women and the uncommitted.

INTRODUCTION

Although it was heralded as one of the year's most spectacular athletic events, ABC's "Wide World of Sports" decided not to bid for the rights to cover the first International Sex Bowl.

The promoters of this carnal contest announced that the competition would feature "eight talented couples, all amateurs, representing the United States, Russia, France, Italy, Great Britain, West Germany, Red China, and South Africa."

Each couple would "compete during four rounds of uninhibited sexual activity."

The men behind the project—Dr. Harrison T. Rogers, a prominent psychologist and speech therapist, and his assistant, Bruce Guido—made it eminently clear that their prime motive in staging the contest to choose the world's champion fornicators was, simply, to make as much money as possible.

Let Masters & Johnson and the folks at the Kinsey Institute concern themselves with the biological, psychological, and sociological implications of relations between men and women. Rogers and Guido were interested only in giving the public the kind of "entertainment" it would pay big bucks to see.

Funded by a group of West Coast businessmen, who had put up $200,000 in seed money, the sporting event was scheduled to be held in New York, with closed-circuit TV cameras carrying the gyrations, grunts, and moans to appreciative paying audiences throughout the world.

1

Each couple entered in the sex olympics had already won semi-final matches in their home countries. Now they would be going up, couple by couple, against each other for the coveted title of the World's Superstars of Sex.

They would be judged on a number of skills and qualities, particularly "finesse, ability to excite, and staying power."

One estimate of the promoter's take from closed-circuit-TV tickets and video-cassette sales exceeded one million dollars.

Dr. Rogers pointed out that golf, football, track and field, basketball, tennis, and baseball stars were handsomely rewarded for their efforts and prowess. At long last, he said, the time had come for the world's most popular participant sport to select its champions and to bestow upon them the honor and recognition they so richly deserve.

The press, understandably, exhibited keen interest in the International Sex Bowl. Wire services, newspapers, magazines, here and in many foreign capitals, vied for interviews with the sponsors of the big event, and the competition for the few press tickets available was fierce.

Although some journalists and columnists condemned the pubic marathon as outrageous, ill-advised, obscene, and tawdry, most media coverage was objective. To the majority of reporters, this unique display of activated genitalia merely reflected society's growing preoccupation with sex, lust and the flesh. Many felt that, with the way things were going it had to happen sooner or later.

As the big evening drew closer, Rogers built up even more interest and suspense by refusing to give the location of the Manhattan hall where the sexcapade would take place. He explained that seating capacity was limited and that he wanted to avoid the likelihood that frenzied mobs would storm the place and demand to be admitted.

In defending the erotic exhibition, Rogers noted, "We want to take sex out of the gutter and put it where it belongs. We're ultimately hoping to make this an annual event, preferably in a large football stadium. Unhappily, we've already been turned down by the Astrodome in Houston, but we're negotiating with sporting interests in more liberal cities."

He continued, "I don't see any reason why it shouldn't be an event in the Summer Olympic games. And someday, possibly in the not too distant future, it could be a marvelous source of revenue for state lotteries and off-track-betting parlors."

2

Just two days before the starting gun was scheduled to set the International Sex Bowl contestants in motion, Rogers called a final press conference. The room was crowded with excited reporters, eager both to interview finalists and to obtain a coveted ticket.

It was a meeting few of them would soon forget.

The International Sex Bowl, Dr. Rogers announced cheerfully, was a hoax — and so was he.

"Rogers" was actually Alan Abel, one of America's foremost hoaxters; the same man who, a few years earlier, had generated reams of international press coverage with his campaign on behalf of SINA, the Society for Indecency to Naked Animals. Despite the apparent contradiction it its name, SINA fought a valiant battle to put clothes on horses, pigs, large dogs, and other four-legged creatures, to protect every pure citizen from the devastating shock of encountering nude Dobermans on the street and bare-rumped elephants in the zoo.

Abel revealed to the stunned (and disappointed) press contingent that he had concocted the International Sex Bowl to publicize a movie he had just produced, *Is There Sex after Death?*

His stunt had worked beyond his highest expectations. Abel's perception of today's sexually hung-up society was right on target. He had found a sensitive spot and manipulated it to achieve his promotional ends.

In truth, America has become a nation immersed in — and obsessed by — all things sexual.

It is a land of pornography shops on a thousand Main Streets.

The movie theatres that used to feature Saturday afternoon kiddie cartoon festivals are now packing 'em in with hard-core films.

Nearly every newsstand is chock full of magazines bulging with four-color illustrations of the human body. The details are explicit beyond belief and the positions displayed are incredibly graphic.

Prime-time network situation comedies are getting laughs with mate swapping, group sex, vasectomies, adultery, and flashing raincoats.

Nearly every new novel has a plethora of obligatory sex scenes.

Publications catering to the specific needs of sadists, masochists, transsexuals, transvestites, exhibitionists, sodom-

3

ists, bisexuals, and bondage and whip aficionados are available from California street-corner vending machines.

Nude beaches are proliferating, and the bathing suits worn by most women today would have branded them as brazen hussies not long ago.

Topless clubs, where men ogle mammary glands in motion, are proliferating from coast to coast, and bottomless clubs are showing voyeurs how the other half lives.

Nearly every city has harlots lurking in doorways, catering to the whims and desires of men out to buy a few moments of groin gratification.

Madison Avenue sells products, not on their merits, but on the sex appeal of the nubile nymphs and macho males in magazine ads and TV commercials.

New "marital aids and novelties" are flooding the marketplace. These dubious devices of pulsating passion appeal to millions of men and women who feel that their own natural equipment is not adequate.

Newspaper gossip columns unashamedly discuss the sexual adventures of movie stars, politicians, and sports figures.

The divorce rate has doubled, and U.S. Government figures show that in this country, once internationally respected for its purity and probity, 1.3 million unmarried persons are now living with members of the opposite sex.

Shere Hite, who had supported her project by working as a nude model for men's "skin" magazines, publishes *The Hite Report*, a study of female sexuality. Three thousand women, ranging in age from 14 to 78, respond to her questionnaire eliciting their thoughts, attitudes, and comments on their sex lives and preferences. Using blunt language, they freely discuss multiple orgasms, masturbation, clitoral stimulation, intercourse positions, fellatio, cunnilingus, sexual fantasies, foreplay, Lesbianism, and frequency of "doing it." Full of four- letter words, many uttered by American mothers, the book quickly climbed to a high spot on the bestseller list.

William Morris, the well-known agent, wouldn't want to represent the performers handled by the agents of erotica — the folks who specialize in spotting and booking the men and women who form the backbone of America's burgeoning live- sex-show industry. In the best tradition of vaudeville, these intrepid talents do two and, if they're up to it, three and four shows a day, all the while demonstrating skills hard to come by.

4

In such national centers of vice and venery as New York and San Francisco, the sexual display is authentic. It's meant to be stimulating, not simulated. The old stag films of our college days seem like Walt Disney features compared to what takes place on the stages of the nation's porn places.

Jazz buffs who buy a new book, *Good Vibrations*, may be disappointed. It's subtitled: *The Vibrator Owner's Manual of Relaxation, Therapy, and Sensual Pleasure*. This guide to the joy of doing it by yourself is advertised in, of all unlikely places, the once staid, gray *New York Times*.

Another recently published tome, *Becoming Orgasmic: A Sexual Growth Program for Women*, has a chapter describing "The Vibrator As a Friend."

Evidently, millions of American women are using this handy new power tool, despite the energy shortage.

But sex toys are not for women only. The men's magazines are full of ads designed to appeal to the man who has everything he needs to meet his need for female companionship except a female.

For these lonely chaps, relief is as close as their nearest mailbox. All it takes is a check or a money order and the girl of their peculiar dreams will be on her way. Actually *girl* is a misnomer; *doll* is more like it. But she's like no Barbie doll you've ever seen!

"Angie" is life size, and most of her is "made of soft, resilient foam. Her skin is soft and silky and warms to the human touch. Her body yields just enough, not too much. You'll love her. She'll love you."

Angie is described as a multitalented helpmate, and unlike the dolls most of us are familiar with, she's anatomically complete. And she's very accommodating—in several places.

The price of this pliant partner? For $69.95, you get the regular Angie doll, with "French," "Greek," and "straight" features. Another ten bucks buys an Angie with an "electronically pulsating vagina."

But if you spring for $89.95, you get a *talking* Angie, fully equipped with a nifty concealed tape player that allows the lucky owner to have her "spur you on to greater heights of sensual expression" and "hear me moan in the ecstasy of repeated climax."

There are many implied advantages to Angie and the host of other pleasure-giving dolls on the market. They're always there

5

when you need them. They add zilch to your food and clothing bills. They can't sue you for alimony or, least of all, for child support. And the only excuse you can expect is "Not tonight, dear. My batteries are dead."

On the other hand, the man in her life can't claim her as a tax deduction.

If that grand old guy with a lamp, Diogenes, thought he was having a rough time looking for an honest man, he would have been thankful that he wasn't around today and searching for a pure maiden in the San Francisco area.

As a newspaper headline put it, "Bay Area Virgins Hard to Find." According to the folks at Planned Parenthood, the girls living in and around San Francisco are, far and away, the most sexually active teenage females in America.

Whereas although 35% percent of the nation's unmarried women between 15 and 19 have "gone all the way," the active-participant rate in San Francisco is 60 percent.

A spokeswoman for Planned Parenthood noted that an increasing number of female teenagers believe that being four to seven months pregnant and wearing maternity clothes is "very much a status symbol."

So, although Tony Bennett left his heart in San Francisco, thousands of girls are losing something else there.

The same nationwide study of twenty-two hundred single young women also revealed that more than half of those who had committed The Act went on to do it again with at least one new partner.

The survey was conducted by two researchers from Johns Hopkins University, who noted that it was extremely unlikely that "exhortations or simplistic tinkering" could change the pattern of teenage sexuality. They concluded, "It is of no little sociological significance that most sexually active young unmarried women in the United States are engaging in that behavior either in their own homes or in the homes of their partners."

Clearly, from coast to coast, the traditional good night kiss has been replaced by something more strenuous.

The marketplace is chock full of sexually-oriented products to amuse and entertain both major sexes:

A pair of men's briefs featuring a four-color illustration of

Pinocchio on the front. In this case the little fellow's nose grows, not when he fibs, but when the wearer's appendage rises to the occasion. A truly unusual conversation piece.

The ladies are offered frilly mood pants, with a heart emblazoned on a central spot. Body temperature causes the sensual symbol to change color, reflecting the wearer's alleged state of passion at the moment.

For those who believe there is a time and a place for everything, a new digital watch would seem to be just the thing. With a mere touch of the button, two key words appear. One of them is, *Let's.*

Mirror, mirror on the ceiling, it's fun to see ourselves peeling. With these mirrors, a couple can bask in their own reflected glory. They enable you to simultaneously be both activists and voyeurs. Mirror, mirror on the wall, oh what fun to watch us ball!

If you've ever wanted to be a literal prisoner of love, you'll appreciate the latest issue of *The Bondage Annual.* You'll find it easy to restrain your joy with this catalog of punitive products. What would life be without body belts, harnesses, gags, training devices, masks, discipline helmets, leather corsets, arm binders, and of course, those old favorites, whips and chastity belts?

When we were kids, lots of young men lifted weights. Now they call it "pumping iron." But the purpose of all that sweating and groaning was to build up those major muscles the deltoids, tricepses, and bicepses.

Today there seems to be tremendous interest in developing another muscle, and all sorts of devices abound to help those less than well endowed add heft, length, and stamina to what writers of poor sex fiction call "the love muscle." Most of these organs builders are suction pumps said to turn the puny into the powerful. One ad boasted these "unsolicited testimonials" from satisfied customers: "Added three inches in 30 days"; "Greatest invention of all times"; and "Added 2″ in length and 1½″ in girth."

Known euphemistically as "peter pumps," they are presented as the big solution for the man with a small problem.

If you still regard women as shy, gentle, unassuming creatures, you'll have a tough time getting a Dallas accountant to share your opinion. He was recently accosted by two attractive young ladies who, at the point of a gun, forced him to drop his trousers and then made him perform wild acts upon their bodies. At last report, police were still trying to track down these man-bites-dog rapists.

First-time visitors to New York, who have been told that it is a cold, unfriendly, unfeeling city, have a pleasant surprise in store for them. To get an accurate picture of what the Big Apple is really like, one only has to turn to the pages of the city's famed journal of sociability and good fellowship, *Screw*. Each week, scores of clearly warm, attractive and compassionate women spend their hard-earned money to attract lonely men so that they may offer them a respite from life's pressures and troubles.

One, a self-admitted "nympho divorcee," advertises her eagerness to meet "a variety of generous men to help overcome loneliness." Free-minded Peggy asks, "Are You New in Town? Don't go to the United Nations. Come see me—I Know All Cultures."

Chris seems to want to bring out the very worst in her boyfriends: "I like nothing better than to have a man treat me like a slave and think of me only as an object on whom he can vent his lust." In case the reader isn't fully convinced that Chris feels she's been a bad girl and should be punished, she adds, "It drives me crazy to have a man use and abuse me both physically and verbally in order to satisfy his most primitive urges. Make me crawl, make me beg, make me grovel at your feet and you will make me come. I want to be your slave. I NEED to be your slave!"

Then, there's Marsha, a girl ready to make both members of the family happy: "BRING YOUR WIFE. When you're out to enjoy the varieties of life, why not consider bringing your wife?

"I'll tantalize her, I'll activate you . . . .

"Swinging with three is more fun than two!"

The needs of the harried businessman are not neglected either. One ad offers an *Executive Box Lunch Special.* Column A features a selection of "12 luscious, beautiful girls," and men who also want to satisfy a less esoteric need may choose a sandwich and beverage from column B.

This unusual catering establishment also thoughtfully provides a "delivery service" for the man who finds it difficult to come himself.

Sex is permeating the pages of our nation's daily newspapers, too. Readers may have been shocked by a recent Associated Press dispatch from Philadelphia: "Honeysuckle Divine, an exotic dancer who uses an unusual technique to play the flute, blow out candles and smoke cigarettes, was arrested last night on a charge of open lewdness after a 35- minute nude performance."

A few days later, it was reported that Ms. Divine, whose real name is Betty Jane Allsup, won a court order allowing her to continue performing in the City of Brotherly Love. But the judge did order the theater to display a sign warning prospective patrons that they would be witnessing "an extreme nude dance."

No detailed description of Honeysuckle Divine's "unusual technique" was given, but astute readers probably hazarded some fascinating guesses.

The headline in the august pages of *The New York Times* read: "SEX RATING AT M.I.T. STIRS FUROR." As the story revealed, two young female undergraduates had conducted a research project the likes of which the venerable Massachusetts Institute of Technology had never seen and would probably never forget.

The ladies became a dynamic dating duo, establishing "relationships" with 36 male students. None of the men suspected that their sexual ability — or lack of it — was of academic interest to the friendly females.

The girls were as copious in notetaking as in coupling. The result was a study, "Consumer Guide to M.I.T. Men," which appeared in a campus newspaper. It offered other female students a critical bed's-eye view of the sexual prowess of each of the unwitting "research subjects."

Since it named names, it caused a good degree of consternation (if not shock) among the now-exposed men, all of whom had been rated with from one to four stars.

The lucky four-star lads were described as "a must. Close your eyes and waves crash, mountains erupt and flowers bloom." But the men on the bottom rung of the lust ladder, the one-star unfortunates, were said to be "recommended in emergencies only."

One of the budding sexologists claimed she was simply interested in showing men "how it feels to be used as a sex object, and to be judged for their sexual performance."

She succeeded.

The neighborhood moviehouse used to be known for family fare, Saturday kiddie-cartoon matinees, and popcorn. And on Saturday nights, young couples may have used their balcony seats to good advantage. But today there is almost always much more action on the screen than in the audience.

The producers of pornographic films are, if nothing else, imaginative in titling their films, such as: *Slippery; Teenage Deviate; All the Way; Velvet Tongue;* and *High Rise.*

The grandmother of all today's porno offerings is *Deep Throat.* As larynx fans will recall, it was the moving story of a woman who had everything, but she had hers in the wrong place.

Deep Throat made a formerly unknown performer, Linda Lovelace, a household name. It established the cult of "porno chic," which saw otherwise respectable men and women flock to theaters throughout the country where they could sit in air-conditioned comfort and watch Ms. Lovelace demonstrate her famed skill.

Many critics found values, socially redeeming and otherwise, in this film — values the producers may not have realized were there. As *Women's Wear Daily* Managing Editor Mort Sheinman pointed out, "There is something for nearly everyone in *Deep Throat,* the inspirational study of a young woman's fight for fulfillment that has been drawing unusual crowds to New York's World Theatre.

"It is a remarkable film, drawing not only on the research of Sigmund Freud but the fables of Wilhelm Jensen in his highly acclaimed 'Gradiva.'" Jerry Gerard, who wrote, edited and directed *Deep Throat* (have we a budding Orson Welles here?), provides a bold thrust forward in the history of contemporary cinema, plunging deeply into areas seldom, if ever, explored on screen."

Mr. Sheinman, a respected film buff, went on to heap additional praise on the film, noting that the poignancy of Ms. Lovelace's plight "and the exultation of her eventual triumph rank with the most moving bits of film in this reviewer's memory."

10

Other critics were equally lavish in their acclaim, and as *Variety* might have put it, *Deep Throat* was Boffo at the Box Office.

The floodgates had been opened even further.

America is obsessed with sex. We talk about it. We tell our friends about it. We think about it. We ask psychiatrists to make it better. We go to the movies to watch it. We sometimes pay a stiff price for it. We read about it. We find ourselves confused by it. We spend thousands of dollars at clinics where our performance is tested, measured, photographed, evaluated, and sometimes laughed at.

We even "do it."

But despite all the advice and counsel being spewed out by today's self-styled authorities, millions of decent men and women are failing in their never-ending quest for a rich, full, satisfying relationship with a person of the other sex.

We've read *The Sensuous Woman*, *The Joy of Sex*, *Everything You've Always Wanted to Know About Sex . . .*, *The Happy Hooker*, and *Portnoy's Complaint*. Still, things aren't going very well. We are not thrilled with our sex lives.

Could it be that we're trying too hard? Is it possible that we're listening to the wrong people? Are today's self-styled experts feeding us drivel?

The plain truth is that the contemporary purveyors of sex manuals, porno films, skin magazines, and erotic machines *are* Johnnies- (and Janes-) come-lately on the sex front.

Our parents and grandparents knew everything that any decent man or woman really needed to know about sex.

The fact that you're here to read this is living proof that they were amply skilled in the techniques of dating, mating, and begetting.

Unlike today's uptight, unsure, insecure, and troubled generation, they were lucky enough to be around during the Golden Age of Sex. It was a time when the authors of sex, marriage, and hygiene books and manuals—most of whom were eminent physicians—dispensed the kind of advice, information, and guidance we so sorely need today.

They laid down simple, easy-to-follow directions, enabling their readers to lead happier, more fulfilling, better-adjusted sex lives.

Thanks to *This Was Sex*, we can return to those glorious days of yesteryear, to a time when sex *was* what it *should be.* Here, in one handy volume, is the sex knowledge and guidance you have been seeking, but have been unable to find until now. Here, taken from the books that shaped a healthier, more rewarding life for millions of Americans is *your* guide to sex, marriage, and morals.

Every word (except for the brief introductory passages) is authentic. Nothing has been changed in this unique effort to put sex where it belongs.

Remember — this was the very best, most authoritative sex counsel available.

Pay attention. And good luck.

MEN AND WOMEN
ARE DIFFERENT

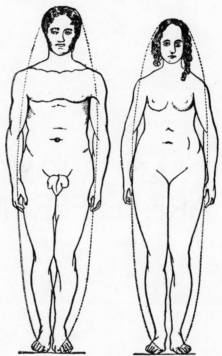

Difference in Form of Man and Woman.

YOU MAY HAVE NOTICED THAT MEN AND WOMEN HAVE DIFFERENT SEXUAL ORGANS. HERE ARE SOME OTHER CHARACTERISTICS THAT SET THEM APART

One must be a mysogynist of very high degree to introduce the pathological notion of imbecility into the evolution of the normal mentality of women.

In reality, the individual differences are much greater in man and woman than the psychological from the physical point of view, so that they render a definition of the average extremely difficult.

We are acquainted with bearded women, athletic women, as well as beardless men and puny men. From the mental point of view, there are also viragos and men with feminine instincts. Imbeciles are not wanting in both sexes, but no reasonable person will deny that an intelligent woman is superior to a narrow-minded man even from the purely intellectual point of view.

In spite of these difficulties, I shall attempt to bring forward the principal points which distinguish, in a general way, the masculine mind from the feminine, relying on my own observations and especially on the mental phenomena of both sexes.

The fundamental difference between the psychology of woman and that of man is constituted by the irradiations of the sexual sphere in the cerebral hemispheres, which constitute what may be called *sexual mentality.*

Adhering in a general way to the main definitions of psychology, we assert that from the purely intellectual point of view, man considerably excels woman in his creative imagination, his faculty for combination and discovery, and by his critical mind.

As regards will power, woman is, in my opinion, on the average superior to man. It is in this psychological domain more than in any other that she will always triumph.

On the average, woman is more artful and more modest; man coarser and more cynical, etc.

[August Forel, M.D., Ph.D., LL.D. (formerly Professor of Psychiatry at and Director of the Insane Asylum in Zurich, Switzerland), *The Sexual Question: A Scientific, Psychological, Hygienic, and Sociological Study for the Cultured Classes* (New York: Rebman, 1908), pp. 67-71.]

LET'S BE GRATEFUL THAT A WOMAN'S SEXUAL DESIRE IS SO SMALL

Love in the man — Undoubtedly man has a much more intense sexual appetite than woman. He loves sensually and is influenced in his choice by physical beauty. In accordance with the nature of this powerful impulse, he is aggressive and violent in his wooing. At the same time this demand of nature does not constitute all of his mental existence. When this longing is satisfied, love temporarily retreats behind other vital and social interests.

Love in the Woman — With a woman it is quite otherwise. If she is normally developed mentally, and well-bred, her sexual desire is small. If this were not so, the whole world would become a brothel and marriage and a family impossible.

It is certain that the man that avoids women and the woman that seeks men are abnormal. Woman is wooed for her favor. She remains passive. This lies in her sexual organization, and is not founded merely on dictates of good breeding.

[Joseph G. Richardson, M.D., Professor of Hygiene, Univ. of Pennsylvania (assisted by 17 other authorities), *Health and Longevity* (1909).]

WOMEN MAY NOT HAVE HUGE BICEPS, BUT THEIR LOVE IS STRONGER THAN YOU MAY THINK

Woman's love is stronger than death; it rises superior to adversity, and towers in sublime beauty above the niggardly selfishness of the world.

Misfortune cannot suppress it; enmity cannot alienate it; temptation cannot enslave it. It is the guardian angel of the nursery and the sick bed; it gives an affectionate concord to the partnership of life and interest; circumstances cannot modify it; it ever remains the same to sweeten existence, to purify the cup of life on the rugged pathway to the grave, and melt to moral pliability the brittle nature of man.

It is the ministering spirit of home, hovering in soothing caresses over the cradle, and the deathbed of the household, and filling up the urn of all its sacred memories.

[Mary R. Melendy, M.D., Ph.D., *Perfect Womanhood for Maidens, Wives, Mothers*—A Book Giving Full Information on All the Mysterious and Complex Matters Pertaining to Women (Boland, 1903), p. 40.]

IF TODAY'S WOMEN ARE AS PUNY, FRAGILE, AND DEGENERATE AS THEY SEEM, THE FAULT LIES WITH THEIR GRANDMOTHERS

The race of womankind today is not as hardy as its grandmothers or great-grandmothers. Why? Perhaps artificialities of civilization have much to do with those who have not learned that natural laws of being are to be preferred.

Gail Hamilton, a woman many years ahead of her generation in thought, wrote:

If the women of today are puny, fragile, degenerate, are they not the grandchildren of their grandmothers, bearing such constitutions as their grandmothers could transmit? It was the duty of

17

THE SWEET GIRL GRADUATE.

those venerable ladies not only to be strong themselves, but to see to it that their children were strong. A sturdy race should leave a sturdy race.

It was far more their duty to give to their children vigorous minds, healthy nerves, firm principles, than it was to spin and weave and make butter and cheese all day. We should have got along just as well with less linen laid up in lavender, and if our grandmothers could only have waited we would have woven them more cloth in a day than their hand looms would turn out in a lifetime.

But there is no royal road to a healthy manhood and womanhood. We should have more reason to be grateful to our ancestors if they had given up their superfluous industries, called off their energy from its perishable object, and let more of their soul and strength flow leisurely in to build up the soul and strength of the generations that were to come after them. Nobody is to blame for being born weak. If this generation of women is feeble compared with its hardy and laborious grandmothers, it is simply because the grandmothers put so much of their vitality, their physical nerve and moral fiber into their churning and spinning that they had but an insufficient quantity left wherewithal to endow their children.

And so they wrought us evil.

[J. H. Greer, M.D., *The Wholesome Woman*—A Home Book of Tokology, Hygiene, and Education for Maidens, Wives, and Mothers (1902).]

THE HEART OF A WOMAN IS HER CHEST

The bosom of the woman, says Berg, is the organ by which she is able to express herself most ingeniously.

Its undulations were always her most expressive and skillful rhetoric.

The bosom represents the woman's language and her poetry, her history and her music, her purity and her longing, her policy and her religion, her worship and her art, her secret and her con-

19

vention, her character and her pride, her consciousness, her magic mirror and her mystery.

The bosom is the central organ of all female ideas, desires and humors.

[Bernard S. Talmey, M.D., *Love: A Treatise on the Science of Sex-attraction* (New York: Eugenics Publishing, 1919, 1933), pp. 151-52.]

THERE IS A VERY GOOD REASON WHY IT IS NATURAL FOR WOMEN TO BE ARTIFICIAL

Secrecy, Tact and Artifice Natural to Women—The female sex is generally accused of being "false" and "deceptive."

This accusation rests on this shadow of truth, that man seeks safety in bold, manly defiance and encounter; while woman is ordained to seek it by art, intrigue, policy, artifice, and stratagems.

Undoubtedly her "Maker" understood Himself when He created her thus reserved, discreet, guarded, self-governed, and politic.

This attribute in her is equally valuable to him, by enabling her often to work with and for him, or rather working both cards; she employing shrewdness and tact, while he uses force. She may, indeed, pervert it to false appearances, even hypocrisy and duplicity; but usually Conscientiousness is larger in woman than in man, which generally does, and always should, prevent its wronging others, while it enables her to reach ends only attainable by tortuous measures.

Hence men love female reserve and discretion much more than bluntness and abruptness.

In its proper place we shall apply this principle to the practical "falsehood" of the female toilet, such as "false" hair, "false" teeth, "false" curls, "false" forms, "false" bosoms, "false" colors, or painting of cheeks and penciling of eyebrows; of all of which the "ladies" of today seem rather proud than ashamed.

Suffice it here that they will find it much better to *be* than merely to make believe. These practical falsehoods do not make

20

them any better mothers, though they originate in an excellent female attribute.

[Prof. O. S. Fowler, (author of "matrimony"; "Offspring and Their Hereditary Endowment"; "The Self-instructor"; and "Amativeness"),*Sexual Science*—Including Manhood, Womanhood, and Their Mutual Interrelations; Love, Its Laws, Power, etc.; Selection, or Mutual Adaptation; Married Life Made Happy; Reproduction and Progenal Endowment; or, Paternity, Maternity, Bearing, Nursing, and Rearing Children: Puberty, Girlhood, etc.; Sexual Ailments Restored, Female Beauty Perpetuated, etc., etc. (National, 1879), pp. 140-41.]

A WOMAN'S INABILITY TO CONCENTRATE IS RELATED TO HER ANTERIOR LOBES

The intellect of man, served by firmer and more developed organs, embraces a wider horizon and yields fruit of a higher order.

While the personal intelligence of woman has less extent and power, it is more subtle and acute. Her vivacity, and the multiplicity of her sensations—probably also the conformation of the anterior lobes of her brain—do not allow her to appreciate exactly the relations of things, their causes and effects.

This accounts for her inferiority in the metaphysical sciences. She has difficulty fixing her attention upon a single object. She is little given to abstraction and generalities, but she seizes marvelously sensible qualities and facts of detail, and in everything which simply requires tact, finesse and taste she is incontestably the superior of man.

[A Physician, *Satan.*]

AT LAST THERE IS SCIENTIFIC SUPPORT FOR THE DOUBLE STANDARD!

A great man, acknowledged by the world as such, like Alexander or Caesar, is not jealous if his wife betrays him with an ordinary mortal. In this case the world sees the stupidi-

"IT IS A MYSTERY—THIS LOVE."

ty of the woman. She is not able to recognize the value of her husband and exposes herself to ridicule.

A great man may, therefore, grieve over the loss of cherished affections. But he will rarely be jealous.

A woman will seldom or never be jealous of the women her husband has consorted with before their marriage. She is not exposed to ridicule through his former love affairs.

He did not marry the others but he did marry her. She was preferred.

Except for the possible impairment of his health and vigor, the more love affairs he had the more the wife is honored.

The man has not been changed by his former love affairs. His wife, consequently, has no palpable reason for resentment and she may pardon her husband's former love affairs without any derogation to their dignity.

Not so man.

The experiments of Waldstein and Ekler show that every sexual union ending in the male ejaculation within the vagina, causes a certain saturation of the female blood with a substance, owing its origin within the male body, which exercises a certain change in the female blood.

These authors have shown by experiments on rabbits that the male sperma within the female organism represents a foreign body in the sense of Abderhalden. When the sperma has entered the blood of the female organism, it produces there a specific ferment.

The blood of a rabbit, 24 hours after copulation, possesses the quality of dialyzation upon testicular tissue. This reaction is positive after every copulation, no matter whether fertilization has taken place or not.

23

JEALOUSY.

Thus a part of the male circulates within the blood of the female, even after copulation without fertilization.

This is the reason why aesthetic and fastidious men refrain from marrying a widow or divorced woman.

This is also the reason why the husband consciously or unconsciously resents his wife's former escapades. This resentment is not jealousy, although it is commonly so called.

Sorrow over his wife's former violated chastity, which conventionality considers as the greatest crime a woman could commit, is not jealousy. He is only grieved that her former impurity has lowered her value.

A woman really gives herself up, soul and body, to her first lover. The virginity of her heart is no longer intact. The fragrance has departed from the rose.

[Talmey, *Love.*]

HOW THEIR ADDICTION TO BONDAGE HAS RESTRICTED WOMEN'S DEVELOPMENT

A large percentage of the female half of the civilization have the trunk of the body ligatured so tightly that a full, deep breath is an impossibility.

The corset is an inheritance from the past for which we are not grateful. The custom of wearing this garment has created a model that few women have strength of mind enough not to follow.

Women are "the weaker sex" because they have made themselves so, the violations of physical law reflecting in the mental and spiritual realm. Miss Willard said this, "Niggardly waists and niggardly brains go together. The emancipation of one will keep place with the other; a ligature at the smallest diameter of the womanly figures means an impoverished blood supply in the brain and may explain why women scream when they see a mouse."

In her lifetime Miss Willard was one of the true students of cause and effect.

Dr. Ellis says: "The practice of tight lacing has done more within the last century toward the physical deterioration of

THE IDEAL FIGURE.

civilized man than have war, pestilence and famine combined."

Dr. Foote says: "Tight lacing is a practice more destructive to health and longevity than tobacco-chewing, liquor-drinking or pork eating."

The German physiologist Somering enumerates ninety-two diseases resulting from corset-wearing.

Dr. Richardson says: "If tomorrow women were placed in all respects on an equality with men, they would remain subject to superior mental and physical force so long as they crippled their physical, vital and mental constitution by this one practice of cultivating, under an atrocious view of what is beautiful, a form of body which reduces physical power and thereby deadens mental capacity."

The Chinese Minister, Wu Ting Fang, said that women who wear corsets cannot bear noble sons. Minister Wu, despite the inborn traditions of his race, has reached a wise conclusion regarding Caucasian dress for women.

Dr. Kitchen says: "The whole civilized world is in bondage to a pernicious habit of dress—practiced by women and countenanced by men. Every woman who has grown up in a corset, no matter how loosely worn, is deformed.

"The first indication that a woman's mind and soul are expanding is when she lays aside her corset."

[Greer, *Wholesome Woman.*]

CONTRARY TO POPULAR BELIEF, THERE IS SOLID EVIDENCE THAT WOMEN DO HAVE A SEXUAL APPETITE

In the sexual act the role of the woman differs from that of the man not only by being passive, but also by the absence of seminal ejaculations.

In spite of this the analogies are considerable.

The erection of the clitoris and its voluptuous sensations, the secretion from the glands of *Bartholin* which resembles ejaculation in the male, the venereal orgasm itself which often exceeds in intensity that of man, are phenomena which establish harmony in sexual connection.

Although the organic phenomenon of the accumulation of

semen in the seminal vesicles is absent in woman, there is produced in the nerve centers, after prolonged abstinence, an accumulation of sexual desire corresponding to that of man.

A married woman confessed to me, when I reproached her for being unfaithful to her husband, that she desired coitus at least once a fortnight, and that when her husband was not there, she took the first comer.

No doubt the sentiments of this woman were hardly feminine, but her sexual appetite was relatively normal.

[Forel, *Sexual Questions*, p. 92.]

SOME HARD FACTS ABOUT WOMAN'S SOFTER BRAIN; OR, WHY SHE'S SO MUCH MORE INCONSISTENT THAN THE SUPERIOR SEX

It is not merely in the organs of generation that Nature has placed the differences between the sexes.

The most obvious anatomical differences are those which relate to the external configuration.

A woman's anatomical peculiarities, no less than her special and periodical function, and the very tendencies of her character, all go to prove that she has not been created to cope with the exigencies of material life, or to place in subjection the hostile elements of the outer world.

In man the substance of the brain has more consistency, more density; in woman, it is softer and less voluminous. She is less given to reflection. Everything which occasions violent emotions troubles and bewilders her.

Man, less sensitive, belongs more to himself for sensibility, while it multiplies our relations with the external world, whenever it passes certain limits, subjugates and delivers us without a guide to all the hazards of passion. So, says J. J. Rousseau, "Woman has more wit and man more genius; woman observes, and man reasons."

In fact, there is far less variety of temperament among women. They seem, in this respect at least, to be cast more in common mold than men.

It would seem that, in the designs of Providence, each man

has to follow the paths of a special destiny, and consequently is endowed with special aptitudes. The common destiny of women does not exact those profound and essential differences among them which are remarked among men.

The temperament of woman exposes her to the most singular inconveniences and inconsistencies. Extreme in good, she is also extreme in evil. She is inconstant and changeable; she "will" and she "won't." She is easily disgusted with that which she has pursued with greatest ardor. She passes from love to hate with prodigious facility. She is full of contradictions and mysteries. Capable of the most heroic actions, she does not shrink from the most atrocious crimes.

Man is more brave, woman more courageous. Moved by a resolute will, man comprehends danger, measures, and faces it. Woman calculates nothing; she sees the end, and will attain it at any price. If she be unskillfully thwarted in her imperious desires, her fickleness is changed to obstinacy; you shall crush her sooner than reduce her.

[A Physician, *Satan.*]

EVEN THOUGH WOMEN AREN'T ALL THAT BRIGHT, THEY DO HAVE GREAT INSTINCTS

Atmospheric influences, temperature, and electricity exert a far more powerful influence upon woman than upon man.

She is in more intimate relation with Nature. Her instincts are stronger, while her personal intelligence is less. She readily achieves many things by instinct at which man arrives less surely by reflection. Man is guided by calculation and personal interest, woman by passion and feeling. Man *sees* the truth, woman *feels* it. Ask advice from a woman, you get a prompt "yes" or "no," but if you force her to analyze the principles of her opinion, she may either ignore them, or give but very poor ones.

[A Physician, *Satan.*]

28

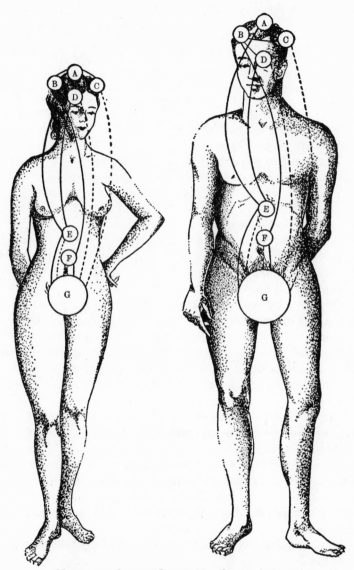

NERVES AND CENTRES CONTROLLING SEXUAL ACTIVITY

A, centre of inhibition in brain; B, centre of libido in brain; C, centre of
voluptas in brain; D, vasodilatory center in medulla oblongata; E, centre of
erection in spinal cord; F, center of ejaculation in lumbar vertebra; G, genital
organs. Solid lines joining nerve centres are centrifugal nerves, broken lines
are centripetal nerves.

IF YOU WANT TO MAKE MEN AND WOMEN WINCE, YOU'VE GOT TO HIT THEM IN TOTALLY DIFFERENT SPOTS

I have rarely met a woman who was painfully embarrassed by any necessary examination of her reproductive organs, while she invariably shrinks and suffers whenever her breasts are seen or handled.

On the other hand, men almost uniformly show embarrassment upon exposure of their organs of generation.

In other words, the pivotal passion of woman is the *maternal.* When you touch her breasts, you "hit her where she lives," and she winces.

This peculiarity is brought into striking relief by a fact well known to every libertine — viz., that even with that terrible dread of pregnancy to restrain her, many a woman consents who will not permit her seducer to touch her breasts.

Man's pivotal passion is the sexual; and when you touch his genital organs, you "hit *him* where he lives," and he winces.

Occasionally we meet a diseased female with excessive animal passion, but such a case is very rare. The average woman has so little sexual desire that if licentiousness depended upon her, uninfluenced by her desire to please man or secure his support, there would be very little sexual excess.

Man is strong — he has all the money and all the facilities for business and pleasure; and woman is not long in learning the road to his favor.

Many prostitutes who take no pleasure in their unclean intimacies not only endure a disgusting life for the favor and means thus gained, but affect intense passion in their sexual contacts because they have learned that such exhibitions gratify men.

I like to think that the strong passion of my mother ·was the maternal.

[Dio Lewis, A.M., M.D. (Author of "Our Digestion; or, My Jolly Friend's Secret"; "Our Girls"; and "Chats with Young Women"), *Chastity; or, Our Secret Sins* (Philadelphia, New York, Boston, Cincinnati, and Chicago: Maclean, 1874), pp. 115-17.]

CHASTITY AND
CONTINENCE

YOU TOO CAN REMAIN CHASTE: A FEW WORDS IN SUPPORT OF PURITY AND SELF-CONTROL

A Chaste Young Life Is Possible. Many are ready to answer in the most positive manner that it is not possible for a young man to live a chaste life. We know that it takes a struggle to do so, but we answer most emphatically that it can be done, and in thousands of cases, it is done.

They have escaped the perils of masturbation and fornication because they were early instructed and cautioned. It is only when a man gives license to his passions that they become regnant and lead him captive at their will.

Don't Judge Others by Yourself. When you hear one declare that no unmarried man can live a continent life, and that in fact all young men have sexual intercourse occasionally before marriage, you may set that man down as an impure man.

He judges others by himself; he associates with young men like himself, snaps his fingers and curls his lip, and says: "They all do it."

He is a liar and libels thousands of pure men who would sooner pluck out the right eye than defile themselves by illicit intercourse.

Thousands Pure. Human nature is sufficiently degraded, and sensuality is sufficiently rampant, but, thank God, all are not vile and impure. There are thousands of men who never know what sexual intercourse is until marriage, and who struggle heroically against their passion and conquer manfully.

There are well-sexed men who never marry and yet live a pure, chaste, continent life to the day of their death.

But if a young man gives reins to his imagination, and associates with vulgar, foul-mouthed companions, whose conversation is principally about women, no wonder that he can not control his passion, for he is pouring oil on the fire all the time.

Dr. Acton's Experience. The following is a statement of Dr. Acton, the noted English surgeon:

"You may be surprised by the statement I am about to make to you, that before my marriage I lived a perfectly continent life. During my university career my passions were very strong, sometimes almost uncontrollable, but I have the satisfaction of thinking I mastered them. It was, however, by great efforts.

"I obliged myself to take violent physical exertion. I was the best oar of my year, and when I felt particularly strong sexual desire I sallied out to take my exercise.

"I was victorious always, and I never committed fornication. You see in what vigorous health I am: it was exercise that saved me."

[Prof. Thomas W. Shannon, A.M., international lecturer; editor, eugenics department, *Uplift* magazine; president, Single Standar Eugenic Movement; author of "Self-Knowledge"; "Perfect Manhood"; "Perfect Womanhood"; "Heredity Explained"; "Guide to Sex Instruction"; etc., *Nature's Secrets Revealed: Scientific Knowledge of the Laws of Sex Life and Heredity; or, Know Thyself*—Vital Information for the Married and Marriageable of All Ages; a Word at the Right Time to the Boy, Girl, Young Man, Young Woman, Husband, Wife, Father, and Mother; Also, Timely Help, Counsel, and Instruction for every Member of Every Home, together with Important Hints on Social Purity, Heredity, Physical Manhood and Womanhood by Noted Specialists, Embracing a Department on Ethics of the Unmarried (Marietta, Ohio: Mullikin, 1914).]

SEX AND THE SPORTING LIFE—THE OLD COACH KNOWS BEST

The moderns who are training are well aware that sexual indulgence wholly unfits them for great feats of strength, and the captain of a boat strictly forbids his crew anything of the sort just previous to a match. Some trainers have gone so far as to assure me that they can discover by a man's style of pulling whether he has committed such a breach of discipline overnight, and have not scrupled to attribute the occasional loss of matches to this cause.

[J. H. Kellog, M.D., *Plain Facts for Old and Young*—Embracing the Natural History and Hygiene of Organic Life (1888).]

ABSTINENCE MAKES THE HEART GROW STRONGER: HOW TAKING IT EASY WITH ONE MUSCLE WILL DO WONDERS FOR THE OTHERS

All eminent physiologists who have written on this point agree that the most precious atoms of the blood enter into the composition of the semen.

A healthy man may occasionally discharge his seed with impunity, but if he chooses—with reference to great physical strength and endurance, as in the pedestrian, boat-racer, prize-fighter or explorer, or with reference to great intellectual and moral work, as in the apostle Paul, Sir Isaac Newton and a thousand other instances—to refrain entirely from sexual pleasure, nature well knows what to do with those precious atoms.

She finds use for them all in building up a keener brain and more vital and enduring nerves and muscles.

[Lewis, **Chastity**, p. 25.]

THE PRICE OF A GIRL'S VIRTUE: EVEN $50,000 ISN'T ENOUGH

Why do young people fall?—A few feeble- minded girls and boys fall because of their inability to appreciate the

34

significance of a fallen condition and for lack of resisting power.

This class is very small compared with the mentally normal fallen class.

Others say, "Girls fall because of the low wages they receive." Here is a young woman. Her clothing is threadbare. She has had nothing to eat for twenty-four hours. She is without a dollar. She does not know where she is to get financial relief. She has moral conviction and character.

A man of millions offers her fifty thousand dollars for sexual favors.

Will she surrender her virtue?

She will scream, scratch, struggle, die before she will voluntarily surrender.

> [Prof. Thomas W. Shannon, *Personal Help for Men*—A Volume of Vital Knowledge Designed to Help Married and Marriageable Men to Avoid the Physical, Mental, and Moral Disasters Due to Ignorance of the Laws of Sexual Nature; Also Advice, Counsel, and Help Essential to Safety and Happiness in the Social Relations of the Sexes, (Marietta, Ohio: Mullikin, 1918), p. 146. (From publisher's preface: "Prof. Shannon became interested in the vital problem of men while still a young man in college. This volume of 'Personal Help for Men' was made possible by a study of men at close range.")]

IF YOU *MUST* FORNICATE, DO IT IN NEW YORK, NEVER IN ALABAMA

The Present Statutes—Fornication

Alabama—If any man and woman live together in adultery or fornication, *each* of them must on first conviction be fined not less than $100, and may also be imprisoned in county jail, or sentenced to hard labor for not more than six months; on second conviction with same person, fine not less than $300 and may also be imprisoned in county jail or sentenced to hard labor for not more than twelve months; and on third conviction or any subsequent convictions with same person, *must* be imprisoned in penitentiary for two years.

Adultery is illicit connection where either is married and includes fornication.

If neither is married, it is fornication; if one married it is fornication for one and adultery for other.

One act of illicit intercourse, and an agreement or consent that it will be repeated if opportunity offers, is sufficient.

District of Columbia—If an unmarried man or woman commit fornication, each of them shall be punished by imprisonment not exceeding six months or by a fine not exceeding $100.

Georgia—Any man and woman who shall live together in a state of adultery or fornication, or of adultery and fornication, or who shall otherwise commit adultery or fornication, shall be severely indicted, and shall be severly punished as for a misdemeanor.

Suspension if they marry.

"If man and woman were in bed together, that would be circumstance that would authorize jury to convict." 7 App. 600.

North Carolina—If any man and woman, not being married to each other, shall lewdly and lasciviously associate; bed and cohabit together, they shall be guilty of a misdemeanor; provided, that the admission or confession of one shall not be received in evidence against the other.

Pennsylvania—If any person shall commit fornication and be thereof convicted, he or she shall be sentenced to pay a fine, not exceeding $100, to the guardians, directors, or overseers of the poor of the city, country or township where the offense was committed, for the use of the poor, and any single woman having a child born of her body, the same shall be sufficient to convict such single woman of fornication.

New York—No Law

[Edith Houghton Hooker, *The Laws of Sex* (Boston: Richard G. Badger, 1921), pp. 150-55.]

WOMEN MUST LEARN TO COPE WITH THE REALIZATION THAT THE SUPPLY OF MALE VIRGINS IS LIMITED

Those who have made a study of the sex instinct in the male seem to think that chastity in normal, healthy men up to the age of thirty or thereabouts is an impossibility, and where it is accomplished it is accomplished at the expense of the physical, mental and sexual health of the individual.

But be it as it may, and leaving disputed questions out of discussion, the fact remains that the vast majority of men of the present day do indulge in sex relations before marriage.

And people that are urging upon our young women to refuse to marry men who have not been perfectly chaste are doing our womanhood a very poor service. As it is now, with all mandom to choose from, there are many, too many, old maids.

With only ten per cent to choose from (because it is admitted that at least 90 per cent of all men have ante-matrimonial relations), what would our women do? They would practically all have to give up any hopes of being married and becoming mothers. And if these ten per cent, who have remained chaste to their married day, were at least a superior class of men in every instance, there would be some compensation in that.

Unfortunately, this is far from being the case, because as all advanced sexologists will tell you, there is generally something wrong with a man who remains absolutely chaste until the age of thirty, thirty-five or forty.

It isn't moral principles in all cases; it is mostly cowardice, or sexual weakness. And sad as it may be to state, these perfectly good, chaste men do not generally make satisfactory husbands, and their wives are not apt to be the happiest ones.

I fully agree with Professor Freud in his statement "that sexual abstinence does not help to build up energetic, independent men of action, original thinkers, bold advocates of freedom and reform, but rather goody-goody weaklings."

[William J. Robinson, M.D. (chief, department of genito-urinary diseases and dermatology, Bronx Hospital Dispensary; editor of the *American Journal of Urology and Sex-*

37

ology; author of "Treatment of Sexual Impotence and Other Sexual Disorders in Men and Women"), "Sexual Problems of Today"; and "Eugenics and Marriage", *Woman: Her Sex and Love Life* (New York: Eugenics Publishing, 1917), pp. 312-13.]

THE OLD BACHELOR AND THE OLD MAID— LET'S GET THEM TOGETHER

There are, no doubt, two kinds of old bachelors, those who are chaste and those who are not.

The old bachelor no doubt leads a less empty existence than the old maid, but the void exists none the less. Man also needs compensation for the absence of love and family, but his brain is more capable than that of woman of finding this compensation in hard intellectual work or in some other employment.

The old bachelor is generally pessimistic and morose. He easily becomes the slave of his fads and hobbies, and the peculiarities of his character are proverbial. His egoism knows no bounds, and his altruistic impulses usually find too few objects or echoes.

The chastity of old bachelors conceals sexual anomalies. But even apart from this, the old celibate easily becomes shy, affected, misanthropic or misogynistic, at least if some energetic friend does not induce him to utilize his power of work in some useful sphere. At other times he lavishes exaggerated admiration on women and worships them in a pompous manner.

In a separate category come those old bachelors who are chaste and celibate for high moral reasons, and whose life is spent in social work, although they are only men and cannot for this reason free themselves from all the peculiarities we have mentioned. In a word, the object of life is partly wanting in the best of old bachelors, and this void not only affects his sentiments but his whole mental being.

His general tendency to pessimism and egoism would be sufficient alone to provoke an energetic protest against the abandonment of social power to celibates.

The old bachelor who is not chaste generally descends to pornography, only becoming acquainted with the worst side of woman. He becomes a misogynist because he wrongly attributes to all women the character of those with whom he has intimate relations.

What we have said of the old bachelors applies in a still more marked degree, to old maids.

Still more than men they have need of compensation for sexual love, to avoid losing their natural qualities and becoming dried-up beings or useless egoists.

But if the void left by love is greater in her, woman possesses such natural energy and perseverance, combined with such great power of devotion, that on the whole she is more capable than man of accomplishing the work which the void in her existence requires. Unfortunately, many women do not understand this.

On the other hand, those who devote themselves to social philanthropic works, to art or literature, to nursing the sick or to other useful occupations, instead of amusing themselves with futile things, may greatly distinguish themselves in social pursuits, and thus obtain real compensation for the loss of love.

As to the old maid who lives alone with her egoism, her whims and fancies generally exceed those of the old bachelor. She has not the faculty of creating anything original by her own intellect, so that, having lost love, all her mental power shrinks up.

Her cat, her little dog, and the daily care of her person and small household occupy her whole mind.

It is not surprising that such persons generally create a pitiable and ridiculous impression.

[Forel, *Sexual Questions*, pp. 127-29.]

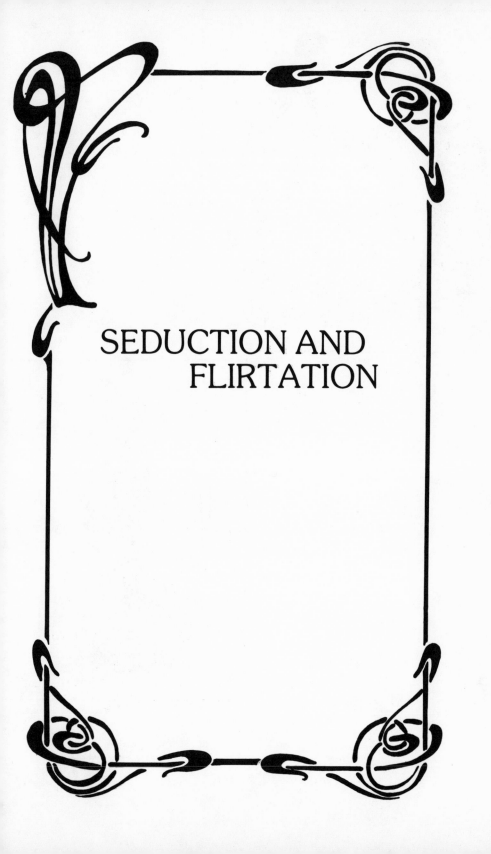

SEDUCTION AND
FLIRTATION

Then

Now

42

IT STARTS WITH SOME LITTLE LIBERTIES, BUT ONLY THE DEVIL KNOWS WHERE IT WILL FINALLY END

The first step usually taken by the young woman on the downward road is the allowance of little liberties on the part of young men.

They may be slight at first, perhaps only a significant pressure of the hand, or the arm placed about the waist, or some similar impropriety. By degrees, slight advances are made along the same line, until the grossest breaches of immodesty are permitted.

We are not overstating the matter when we say that we have met many young women who have been led into wrong- doing, who have confessed that this was the beginning of their downward course.

[Kellog, *Plain Facts.*]

YOUNG WOMEN OF AMERICA, LISTEN CAREFULLY!

Young women of America, if you knew how lightly you are estimated by those who so earnestly and passionately seek your favors, you would certainly deny them, if the effort cost your lives.

43

A TYPICAL LIBERTINE.

There are degrees in libertinism, the affectionate caress, the want on impropriety, the deliberate seduction; and, however humiliating the assertion may be, it is nevertheless a fact, that these several stages are at the command of him to whom you surrender the outposts of your purity. The world is full of maxims which demonstrate the truth of this. "If a woman hesitates, she is lost"; "C'est le premier pas qui coute," and this sentiment is multiplied into all languages, held by all nations.

The thought that you are deliberately surrendering yourself to the power of any man, is so startling that, if you believed it, you would be well-nigh exempt from danger; for you would certainly guard the fortress with a vigilance that no strategy could surprise.

[A Physician, *Satan.*]

44

SURE, MOST FLIRTS ARE WOMEN— BUT MEN ARE EVEN MORE DETESTABLE!

We cannot find language sufficiently emphatic to express proper condemnation of one of the most popular forms of amusement indulged in at the present day in this country, under the guise of innocent association of the sexes.

We have not the slightest hesitation in pronouncing flirtation pernicious in the extreme.

It may be true, and undoubtedly is the case, that by far the greater share of the guilt of flirtation lies at the door of the female sex; but there do exist such detestable creatures as male flirts.

In nine cases out of ten, he is a rake as well.

His object in flirting is to gratify a mean propensity at the expense of those who are pure and unsophisticated.

He is skilled in the arts of fascination and intrigue. Slowly he winds his coils about his victim, and before she is aware of his real character, she has lost her own.

Such wretches ought to be punished in a purgatory by themselves, made seven times hotter than for ordinary criminals.

Society is full of these lecherous villains. They insinuate themselves in the drawing rooms of the most respectable families; they are always on hand at social gatherings of every sort. They haunt the ballroom, the theatre and even the church when they can forward their infamous plans by seeming to be pious. Not infrequently they are well supplied with a stock of pious cant, which they employ on occasion to make an impression.

They are the sharks of society, and often seize in their voracious maws the fairest and brightest ornaments of a community.

The male flirt is a monster.

Every man ought to despise him; and every woman ought to spurn him as a loathsome social leper.

[Kellog, *Plain Facts.*]

IT OFTEN STARTS WITH A SIX-PACK AND ENDS UP BETWEEN THE SHEETS

The abuse of spirituous liquors is pre-eminently one of the leading factors which promote licentiousness, and the reason is not far to seek—for alcohol notably enfeebles the powers of resistance, confuses the reason, and at the same time awakens and stimulates the desire for sexual gratification by allowing the lower animal passions to transcend the higher.

No healthy person is benefited by the use of any fermented or distilled drink, and probably the habitual use of any liquor which contains alcohol is injurious to the normal person.

Alcoholic beverages are especially dangerous to the Anglo-Saxon and the Celt, since the tendency in these races is to rashly increase the amount of alcohol until moderation is set aside.

Medicinally the stimulants are invaluable, and they have been called "the milk of old people"; but at best they are sharp-edged tools and quite unsuitable for the ordinary individual.

Not to enter into an elaborate discussion, there can, however, be no dispute that the saloons are the disseminators of everything obscene and impure, and the very lighthouses of hell.

[James Foster Scott, M.D. (former obstetrician to Columbia Hospital for Women and Lying-in Asylum, Washington, D.C.), *The Sexual Instinct*—Its Use and Dangers As Affecting Heredity and Morals; Essentials to the Welfare of the Individual and the Future of the Race (New York: E. B. Treat, 1898, 1907), p. 147.]

THE JOY OF COVETING

No words in our vocabulary can adequately express the depths of depravity to which a man must descend before he deliberately can plan and contrive to win the affections of another man's wife.

If possible, there is still a deeper depth of depravity to which some men descend.

46

We refer to the vilest of the vile—to men who will resort to every possible means to lead the husbandless and the fatherless astray.

Perhaps some reader may reply: "I would not take the virtue of a pure woman: I seek pleasure only with women who are fallen."

Every such woman is some mother's girl. She was once as pure as your wife, sister or mother. Some fond father once dandled her on his knee and proudly called her "darling."

Does a reader reply: "She has brought on her own social disgrace and voluntarily has placed her body on the market; therefore, I am not responsible for her sin."

If you could hear the pathetic story of her fall; how she fell in mere childhood, before she knew the name of the act or what it involved; or how being feeble-minded, she lacked resisting power; or how some well-dressed and accomplished seducer, under solemn promise of marriage, oft repeated, seduced and ruined her; if you could appreciate her enforced exclusion from society and home, discarded by her parents, brother and sister; if you could feel the anguish of her degraded, pentinent soul at the close of a life of shame, you would be a fallen woman's friend and seek to restore her to a life of purity instead of helping to sink her into deeper depths of hopeless ruin.

[Shannon, *Personal Helps*, pp. 137-38.]

HOW TO WIN A MAN'S HEART: FIRST YOU STEAL A LIZARD . . . .

As women are not allowed to make Love actively, they resort to various cunning arts with which they indirectly reach the hard hearts of men.

Magic is the most potent of these arts, and always has been so considered by women; for, curiously enough, one finds on looking over the folklore of various nations, ancient and modern, that in nineteen cases out of twenty where a Love- charm is spoken of, it is one used by women to win the affection of men.

Probably the real reason why the vast majority of women are so curiously indifferent to the hygienic arts of increasing and

ENMESHED IN CUPIDS BONDS OF INVISIBLE INFLUENCES.

preserving Personal Beauty—as shown in their devotion to tight-lacing, their aversion to fresh air, sunshine, and brisk exercise—is because they know they can infallibly win a man's Love by the use of some simple powder or potion.

In medieval times Personal Beauty was such a rare thing, and created such havoc among men, that the unhappy possessors of it were frequently accused of using forbidden Love-charms, and burnt at the stake as witches.

Today, thanks to our superior sanitary and educational arrangements, Beauty is such a common affair that it has lost all its effect on the masculine heart; hence girls should carefully note a few of the ways by which a man may be irresistibly fascinated.

Italian girls practice the following method: A lizard is caught, drowned in wine, dried in the sun and reduced to powder, some of which is thrown on the obdurate man, who thenceforth is theirs for evermore.

A favorite Slavonic device is to cut the finger, let a few drops of her blood run into a glass of beer, and make the adored man drink it unknowingly. The same method is current in Hesse and Oldenburg, according to Dr. Ploss.

In Bohemia, the girl who is afraid to wound her finger may substitute a few drops of bat's blood.

Cases are known where invocations to the moon were followed by the bestowal of true Love. And if a girl will address the new moon as follows —

> "All hail to thee, moon! All hail to thee!
> Prithee, good moon, reveal to me
> This night who my husband shall be,"

she will dream of him that very night.

A four-leaved clover secretly placed in a man's shoes will make him the devoted lover of the woman who puts it in.

If a girl sees a man washing his hands — say at a picnic — and lends him her apron or handkerchief to dry them, he will forthwith declare himself her amorous slave to eternity.

[Henry T. Finck, *Romantic Love and Personal Beauty* (New York, Macmillan, 1887), pp. 250-51.]

WHAT HAPPENS WHEN A FAST YOUNG WOMAN TEAMS UP WITH A FAST YOUNG MAN?

Some young women, like a certain class of young men, imagine that there is something particularly smart in being fast.

A walk, a ride, or a waltz with some fast young man, perhaps a notorious rake, is an adventure which has a peculiar fascination. They delight in these escapades and adventures which startle old-fashioned people who still have some sense of propriety. What is the consequence?

These young women soon find their moral sense so blunted, that before they are aware of it, they are led to the commission of acts which, but a short time before, they would have regarded

ASPHALT ARABS
How some girls are deceived

with the greatest horror.

In an unguarded moment, the fatal step is taken, and modesty, purity, and honor, all that a woman holds most sacred, are sacrificed, and they are rapidly swept away into the maelstrom of vice.

[Kellog, *Plain Facts.*]

THEY SHOULD PUT A NOOSE ON MEN
WHO SEDUCE!

Seducers—the Worst Beings on Earth Blasted be that fiend, in human shape, who does this wicked deed!

Hurled, ay, even hunted from society; scorned by man and spurned by woman; uncheered by one ray of love! The plagues of Egypt be upon him, with the mark of Cain, and blasts of sirocco!

Compared with his crime, murder is innocence. Even hanging forever would be too good for him.

And he is thus forever hung, and in a perpetual hell on earth, the fagots and brimstone of whose flames he himself has piled and lighted; while from the heaven of love, and all its joys, he has forever excluded himself.

The raging fires of this diabolical passion are lit up all around him, and all within him. Pestilence is in his very breath.

Moral stench is his only atmosphere, and gross sensuality his perpetual wallowing-place. A living purgatory within and without is his endless portion; because that very blackness of depravity which can ruin an unsuspecting woman is his deepest sin and suffering.

Society has an undoubted right to inflict on him any and all the punishments it may rightfully inflict on any. For such, hanging is by far too good.

Indians should be paid to torture him in his life, and the prince of satanic torturers throughout the next.

THE SAME SWEET, OLD STORY.

Confidence-men, robbers, swindlers, even murderers, are nowhere in comparison.

Public opinion must protect females by inflicting its direst penalties on this most execrable bandit, from whose seductive wiles the best of women are hardly safe.

They prowl, wolf-like, about every neighborhood and family, seeking, by that taking bait of pretended courtship and marriage, to devour all female virtue, and make such terrible havoc.

[Fowler, *Sexual Science*, pp. 326-29.]

THE SIGHT OF A WOMAN'S PLUNGING NECKLINE MAY INCITE A MAN TO PLUNGE RIGHT IN

Young men are not always responsible for spooning.

Some young women take the initiative. Girls who are addicted to the dance are accustomed to free personal contact with men.

These girls are many times inclined to bestow favors. They sometimes invite familiarities. Girls who keep a quantity of vicious postcards in their parlors and who invite their men friends to look at them do not object to spooning.

Girls who are fond of wearing very low-necked dresses certainly ought to be informed that this is the most extreme and dangerous form of invitation. The partially concealed charms of women are universal temptations to men.

A woman has no more moral right to dress in such manner as will excite in men wrong desire, than a man has to tempt a woman to do wrong.

A reform in low-necked dresses is a moral necessity.

[Shannon, *Personal Help.*]

52

ADVICE TO GIRLS:
DON'T YOU DO IT!

Temptations. Fortunate are you, my young girl friend, if you come from a well-sheltered home, if you have been properly brought up, if you have a good and wise mother who knows how to take care of you. A mother's wise counsel given at the proper time, and her comradeship all the time, are more invulnerable than an armor of bronze and more secure than locked doors and barred windows.

But if you have lost your mother at an early age, or if your mother is not of the right sort—it is no use hiding the fact that some mothers are not what they should be—if you have to shift for yourself, if you have to work in a shop, in an office, and particularly if you live alone and not with your parents, then temptation in the shape of men, young and old, will encounter you at every step; they will swarm about you like flies about a lump of sugar; they will stick you like bees to a bunch of honeysuckle.

I do not want you to get the false idea that all men or most men are bad and mean, and are constantly on the lookout to ruin young girls.

No. Most men are good and honorable and too conscientious to ruin a young life.

But there are some men, young and old, who are devoid of a conscience, who are so egotistic that their personal pleasure is their only guide of conduct. They will pester you. Some will lyingly claim that they are in love with you; some perhaps will sincerely believe that they are in love with you, mistaking a temporary passion for the sacred feeling of love.

Some will even promise to marry you—some making the promise in sincerity, others with the deliberate intent to deceive. Still others will try to convince you that chastity is an old superstition, and that there is nothing wrong in sexual relations.

In short, all ways and means will be employed by those men to induce you to enter into sexual relations with them.
Don't you do it!

[Robinson, *Woman,* pp. 262-63.]

THERE ARE TIMES WHEN A WOMAN'S
"NO-NO" MAY BE A "YES-YES!"

The dualism of woman in her first experiences of sexual life is no less dangerous to men.

For the lover, in individual cases, it is difficult, if not impossible, to decide whether the girl's resistance to his wishes is stimulated or sincere; whether her flight is in truth significant of refusal, or whether it really indicates a delicate form of excitement; whether the use of a certain degree of violence will arouse the most ardent passion of love, or the most furious anger; whether his acts will lead him to the most intense erotic joy, or will result in an accusation of rape; whether he will find himself in paradise or in the penitentiary.

This dualism of woman puts man in a dreadful dilemma.

Every lawyer knows with what circumspection must usually be considered all accusations of rape, and what extreme care has to be exercised in such cases if we are to avoid the danger of committing a judicial murder.

More than half of all accusations of rape break down on close enquiry, and are dismissed as false. In many cases, when the legal enquiry is held, examination will show, either that the alleged rape cannot possibly have taken place, or else that the girl was a consenting party.[1]

1. The accusation breaks down for the former reason when medical examination shows beyond dispute that the girl who brings the charge of rape is still an intact virgin.

This happens more frequently than those imagine who are unacquainted with this department of medical jurisprudence. As an example of the second order of events may be a mentioned a case well known in legal circles.

In the law court, bringing an accusation of rape, appeared a very tall girl , while the accused was a man of diminutive stature. The girl deposed that the offense had been committed by day, in a stable, and in the standing posture. A glance at the difference between the height of the two sufficed to show that the thing was physically impossible.

When the girl's attention was called to this impossibility in her story, there slippped out the admission that she had, in fact, stooped down a little.

[Robert Michaels, *Sexual Ethics: A Study of Borderland Questions* (New York: Scribner, 1914), pp. 125-26.]

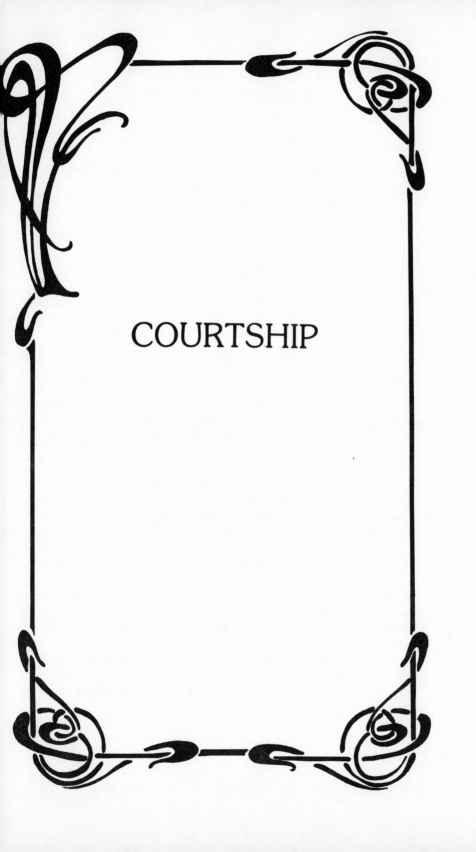

COURTSHIP

SOCIETY HAS A NAME FOR MEN WHO ANSWER THE QUESTION "DID YOU GET ANY LAST NIGHT?"

It is only the most arrant coxcomb who will boast of the favor shown him by a lady, speak of her by her first name, or allow others to jest with him upon his friendship or admiration for her.

[Cecil B. Hartley, *The Gentlemen's Book of Etiquette and Manual of Politeness (1873).*]

A GOOD WOMAN WILL LOVE A HOMELY MAN

Women naturally love courage, force and firmness in man. The ideal man in a woman's eye must be heroic and brave. Woman naturally despises a coward, and she has little or no respect for a bashful man.

Large Men — Women naturally love men of strength, size and fine physique, a tall, large and strong man rather than a short, small and weak man. A woman always pities a weakly man, but rarely ever has any love for him.

Generosity — Woman generally loves a generous man. Religion absorbs a great amount of money in temples, churches, ministerial salaries, etc., and ambition and appetite absorb countless millions, yet woman receives more gifts from man than all these combined: she loves a generous giver. *Generosity* and *Gallantry* are the jewels which she most admires.

A woman receiving presents from a man implies that she will pay him back in love, and the woman who accepts a man's presents and does not respect him, commits an unforgivable wrong.

56

Intelligence—Above all other qualities in man, woman admires his intelligence. Intelligence is man's woman-captivating card.

Soft Men—All women despise soft and silly men more than all other defects in their character. Woman never can love a man whose conversation is flat and insipid. Every man seeking woman's appreciation or love should always endeavor to show his intelligence and manifest an interest in the various topics of the day.

WOMEN LOVE
"HE" MEN

Homely Men—Are admired by women if they are large, strong, vigorous and intelligent. Looks are trifles compared with the other qualities which man may possess.

[B. G. Jefferis, M.D., Ph.D., and J. L. Nichola, A.M., *Safe Counsel; or, Practical Eugenics* (Chicago: Franklin' 1928).]

MEN LOVE WOMEN WHO HAVE A BIG PELVIS AND SMALL FEET. THEY ALSO LIKE SOME OTHER THINGS ABOUT THEM

What Men Love in Women

Female Beauty—Men love beautiful women, for women's beauty is the highest type of all beauty. A handsome woman needs no diamonds, no silks nor satins; her face outshines diamonds and her form is beautiful in calico.

A Good Female Body—No weakly, poor-bodied woman can draw a man's love like a strong, well developed body. A round, plump figure with an overflow of animal life is the woman most commonly sought, for nature in man craves for the strong qualities in women, as the health and life of offspring depend upon physical qualities of wife and mother. A good body and vigorous health, therefore, become indispensable to female beauty.

Broad Hips—A woman with a large pelvis has a superior and significant appearance, while a narrow pelvis always indicates. weak sexuality. The other portions of the body however must be in harmony with the size and breadth of the hips.

Small Feet—Small feet and small ankles are very attractive, because they are in harmony with a perfect female form, and men admire perfection. Small feet and ankles indicate modesty

58

and reserve, while large feet and ankles indicate coarseness, physical power, authority, predominance. Feet and ankles, however, must be in harmony with the body, as small feet and small ankles on a large woman would be out of proportion and consequently not beautiful.

[Jefferis and Nichols, *Safe Counsel.*]

IMPROPER KISSING CAN CAUSE A PAIN
IN THE EAR

How to Kiss.
Kissing comes by instinct, and yet it is an art which few understand properly.

A lover should not hold his bride by the ears in kissing her, as appears to have been customary at Scotch weddings of the last century.

A more graceful way, and quite as effective in preventing the bride from "getting away," is to put your right arm round her neck, you fingers under her chin, raise the chin, and then gently but firmly press your lips on hers.

After a few repetitions she will find out it doesn't hurt, and become as gentle as a lamb.

The word *adoration* is derived from kissing. It means literally to apply to the mouth. Therefore girls should beware of philologists who may ask them with seemingly harmless intent, "May I adore you?"

[Finck, *Romantic Love*, pp. 237-38.]

WHY UGLY GIRLS ARE SO DARN SMART

It is easy to explain how the absurd and fatal notion that intellectual application mars women's peculiar beauty and lessens the feminine graces in general must have arisen.

The inference seems to follow logically from the two undeniable premises that pretty girls very often *are* insipid, and intellectual women commonly *are* plain. But this is only another case of putting the cart before the horse.

Pretty girls, on the one hand, are so rare that they are almost sure to be spoiled by flattery. They receive so much attention that they have no time for study; and ambitious mothers take them into society prematurely, where they get married before their intellectual capacities — which sometimes are excellent — have had time to unfold.

Ugly girls, on the other hand, being neglected by the men, have to while away their time with books, music, art, etc., and thus they become bright and entertaining.

Therefore it is not the intellect that makes them ugly, but the ugliness that makes them intellectual.

[Finck, *Romantic Love*, pp. 154-55.]

BAD THINGS HAPPEN TO UNMARRIED SPOONERS. USUALLY THEIR LIVES ARE BLIGHTED AND THEIR HOMES WRECKED

Should the unmarried spoon?

In the human family, spooning belongs only to the married life.

If indulged in by married people beyond reasonable limits, it leads to sensuality, physical, mental and moral injury.

If indulged in, even to a very limited extent among the single, it is fraught with gravest temptations.

True love will find expression. Intelligent love, love guided by moral convictions, will find the channels of expression that are safe. If young people would meet each other at the marriage altar with unkissed lips, there would be few blighted lives and wrecked homes.

TRUE BLISS.

While a goodbye kiss might be indulged in occasionally near the end of an engagement, by pure minded people without any apparent harm, it is not necessary to their happiness or a necessary expression of love.

[Shannon, *Nature's Secrets*, p. 121.]

SOME MEN DEVISE INSIDIOUS TESTS TO MEASURE A YOUNG WOMAN'S MORAL CHARACTER. THEY ARE WRONG IN DOING SO

TALKING THINGS OVER *before* MARRIAGE

Whether a young man has kept his virtue or not, if he has any sense of respectability left, he is at least selfishly concerned about the virtue of the woman he expects to marry.

Unfortunately, some men have been so trained that they believe they are justified, during courtship, in engaging in exciting familiarities to determine whether or not their sweethearts would be willing to yield.

Such tests are morally wrong, debasing in principle and ungentlemanly.

Only men who are densely ignorant or low in their ideals will stoop to such methods.

Purity, in either men or women, is expressed in the look of the eye, features, tone of conversation, deportment and the company one keeps.

[Shannon, *Personal Help*, p. 153.]

WHAT TURNS A WOMAN ON—OR OFF

Strength and skill in man are the ideal of the young savage and uncultured girl, his intellectual and moral superiority that of the young cultivated girl.

As a rule women are much more the slaves of their instincts and habits than men. In primitive peoples, hardiness and boldness in men were qualities which made for success. This explains why, even at the present day, the boldest and most audacious Don Juans excite most strongly the sexual desires of women, and succeed in turning the heads of most young girls, in spite of their worst faults in other respects.

Nothing is more repugnant to the feminine instinct than timidity and awkwardness in man. In our time women become more and more enthusiastic over the intellectual superiority of man, which excites their desire. Without being indifferent to it, simple bodily beauty in man excites the appetite of women to a less extent.

It is astonishing to see to what point women often become enamored of old, ugly or deformed men.

While the normal man is generally attracted to coitus by

63

nearly every more-or-less young and healthy woman, this is by no means the case in the normal woman with regard to man.

The instinct of procreation is much stronger in woman than in man, and is combined with the desire to give herself passively, to play the part of one who devotes herself, who is conquered, mastered and subjugated.

These negative aspirations form part of the normal sexual appetite of woman.

[Forel, *Sexual Questions*, pp. 93-94.]

LONG ENGAGEMENTS CAN DRIVE A MAN TO EVIL DEEDS

I knew a young man who was plighted to a beautiful and amiable girl, who in spite of her affection, desired to prolong the engagement.

The lovers met every evening, and, like all ardent couples, they caressed each other with delightful fervor. But the intense amatory excitement which these endearments caused in the young man's nervous organization merged after a time into a state approaching madness.

He besought the girl to hasten the day of their union; but she, like many of her sex, believed that courtship is the happiest time of a woman's life; and though no pecuniary obstacles stood in the way of immediate marriage, she desired to postpone the wedding for several more months.

At length the raging passion of the lover, which was concentrated in a vehement desire to possess his future bride, broke all bands of restraint, and being unable to consummate this uncontrollable love with the maiden whom he dearly loved, he was sorely tempted to ease his torments of body and mind by resorting to a public woman of the town.

For a while he strove against the temptation; but at last, in a kind of libidinous frenzy, he yielded.

This lapse from his code of morality, though it gave him a certain relief, began to rack his conscience. Eventually he con-

64

fessed his defection to his fiancee, who from that moment indignantly repudiated him as her lover. The grief of this rejection, added to his past suffering, gave rise to utter recklessness in the young man, and he became a habitual associate of light women.

Such instances as the above are by no means rare.

[Geoffrey Mortimer, *Chapters on Human Love* (London: University Press, 1900), pp. 239-40.]

THE LOOK OF LOVE.
IT'S ALL IN THE LIPS

Beauty of face consists chiefly of expression, which love redoubles, by increasing the action of the faculties.

Active love lights up even plain features with a glow, a warmth, a flush, which loving eyes in the beholder still magnify; so that those in love always think their loved one good-looking.

But reversed love gives even handsome features either a sad and pitiable, or else a fierce and hardened look, which pains and repels.

A hearty sexuality gives a beautiful form and face, to which

THE CHILDLESS LOVER OF CHILDREN.

THE DEVOTED WIFE AND MOTHER.

NO. 210. — AMATIVENESS SMALL.

NO. 211. — CONJUGAL LOVE FULL, PARENTAL VERY LARGE.

65

220. — THE LOOK OF LOVE.

love superadds a radiance really captivating. No face can ever be worth a second look when saddened by disappointment. Love draws all the facial lines upwards, while reversed love draws all downwards.

Active love irradiates the whole face with its sweetest smiles, and suffuses the loving maiden's with a blush most adorning and captivating, even angelic, and far beyond all art to imitate, as seen in the accompanying engraving of well- sexed Caddie in a loving mood; while reversed love chases away all smiles, leaves

THE HARDENED FROWN OF REVERSED LOVE.

THE LAUGH OF LOVE.

a painful blank, or that care-worn, disconsolate, forlorn, pensive look, as if every friend were dead, and death was coveted as a boon.

Contrast the cheek of that blooming maiden, thoroughly in love, with the bloodless cheek of "love deferred," or engraving 210 with 220.

Paradise and purgatory are not more opposite. In love, the full lips quiver with gushing affection, but these same lips, after disappointment, become parched, shrivelled, and inexpressive.

Let this engraving speak to the eye. See that merry, laughing, jubilant face, with love side up.

Just turn this very page bottom side up, and see how cross and fierce the same nose, mouth, cheeks, chin and expression, after the affections have been reversed!

Sexual Science Including Manhood, Womanhood, and Their Mutual Interrelations; Love, Its Laws, Power Etc. By Prof. O.S. Fowler. 1879.

MEN WHO HAVE BEEN SHORT-CHANGED BY NATURE ARE NOT POPULAR WITH FASHIONABLE WOMEN

Woman loves size and physical stamina in men.

Try this experiment:

Place yourself a few feet behind a little, short, brisk, frisking Mr. Bantam, on the fashionable promenade, frequented by women who have learned to "take the measure of a man" at first sight; so that, as they pass him, you, by following right after, can read in their faces just what they think of him; and you will see a petting, babying expression, mingled with a derisive smile, as if thinking, —

What a little bit of a husband that bantam fellow would make, though. He is too large for a cradle, but too small for a bed.

Next, follow a large, tall, prominent-featured, dark- complexioned man, and mark how, when looking at him, their eyes dilate, their mouths distend, and their cheeks suffuse with special admiration!

Other things the same, women love tall men much better than short, because better sexed.

[Fowler, *Sexual Science.*]

A REAL MAN NEVER BACKS DOWN AND IS ALWAYS RIGHT— ESPECIALLY WHEN HE'S WRONG

Woman loves firmness, force and courage in man.

So, young courter, never give up beaten. When you court, at least show game and pluck.

Never confess yourself worsted.

Threaten if you like, but never snivel, nor crave sympathy of any woman, unless you are willing she despise you.

Never "back down" from any position once taken. Much better take right ground at first, but *stick well* to whatever you do assume; for, singular, but true, any genuine woman had rather see her favorite stick to his text, though he, she, and all know him to be in the wrong, than to own up fallible.

A Southern lady once said of a man who perfectly worshipped her, and almost died of a broken heart in consequence of her dismissal,—

> *I dismissed him because he coincided with whatever I said, and had no independent mind and will of his own.*

[Fowler, *Sexual Science.*]

68

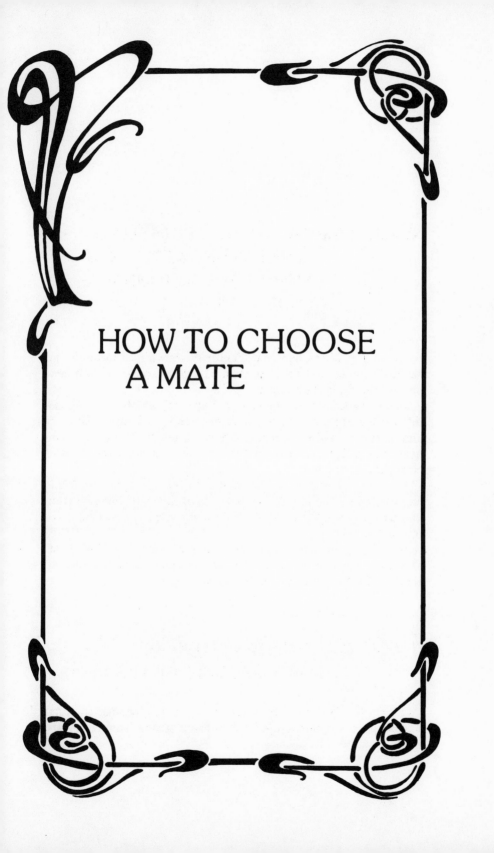

HOW TO CHOOSE
A MATE

NEVER MARRY A MAN WHO PUTS SLUGS IN THE PARKING METER OR EXHIBITS OTHER CRIMINAL TENDENCIES

It has been satisfactorily shown by thorough and scientific investigation that criminals often receive their evil proclivities from their parents.

What are known as the criminal classes, which are responsible for the greater part of the crime committed, are constantly and greatly on the increase. There is no doubt but that inheritance is largely responsible for the continued increase of crime and criminals.

A drunkard begets in his child a thirst for liquor, which is augmented by the mother's use of ale or lager during gestation and nursing, and the child enters the world with a natural taste for intoxicants.

A thief transmits to his offspring a secretive, dishonest, sneaking disposition; and the child comes into the world ticketed for the State prison by the nearest route.

[Kellog, *Plain Facts.*]

IT WOULD BE A MISTAKE TO MARRY A FOP—ESPECIALLY IF HE DRINKS

We wish to warn every young woman against choosing for a husband a man who has a strong leaning toward

70

infidelity; who does not believe in human responsibility; who makes a mock of religion; who is addicted to profanity; who is either grossly intemperate or given to moderate tippling, be it ever so little, so long as he does not believe in and practice total abstinence; who uses tobacco; who is a jockey, a fop, a loafer, a scheming dreamer, or a speculator; who is known to be unchaste, or who has led a licentious life.

[Kellog, *Plain Facts.*]

DO YOU LOVE MR. OR MS. RIGHT
FOR THE WRONG REASONS?

Do You Love Her — because she goes to the altar with her head full of book learning, her hands of no earthly use, save for the piano and brush; because she has no conception of the duties and responsibilities of a wife; because she hates housework, hates its everlasting routine and ever recurring duties; because she hates children and will adopt every means to evade motherhood; because she loves her ease, loves to have her will supreme, loves, oh how well, to be free to go and come, to let the days slip idly by, to be absolved from all responsibility, to live without labor, without care? Will you love her selfish, shirking, calculating nature after twenty years of close companionship?

Do You Love Him — because he is a man, and therefore, no matter how weak mentally, morally or physically he may be, he has vested in him the power to save you from the ignominy of an old maid's existence? Because you would rather be Mrs. Nobody than make the effort to be Miss Somebody? Because you have a great empty place in your head and heart that nothing but a man can fill? Because you feel you cannot live without him? God grant the time may never come when you cannot live with him.

[Jefferis and Nichols, *Safe Counsel.*]

71

A UTERINE WOMAN SHOULD NEVER MARRY A PHALLIC MAN. AND OF COURSE, AN ORCHITIC MAN SHOULD CERTAINLY NEVER EVEN THINK OF MARRYING A CLITORID WOMAN

Two fundamental types of women are outlined by Meador, the uterine and the clitorid.

The uterine is the maternal type, the woman we know, the woman we respect, court, pay homage to, the woman we marry. They constitute the vast class of womanhood and motherhood. They mate with the men of their choice, radiate charm and fascination, and their consuming desire is to make their husbands happy. They are our devoted wives and mothers.

But there is also the clitorid, or sexual type of women.

They soon tire of their husbands. The whole matrix of their life is the physical and the lust for variety. There is hardly any need to dwell on the domestic discord of such women. They are always in search of new romantic adventures.

Woe to the man who marries a clitorid type of woman.

As noted before, fortunate for American family organization, such women are in a very small minority.

Recently, Rene Guyon suggested in his book, *Sex Life and Sex Ethics*, the classification of men into the orchitic and the phallic type, and the classification has been accepted by all sexologists. The orchitic man corresponds to the uterine type of woman. The orchitic men are those who love and are loyal to their wives without any complicated sexual desire. Normal coitus alone appeals to them. They are the husbands and fathers who not only have no need for variation, but view extramarital relationship as criminal, and even repulsive.

The phallic type of man is exactly like the clitorid woman. In both the greatest satisfaction in life is sexual congress with anyone to whom they are not married.

The phallic type of man is in fact a more serious destruction to married happiness than is the clitorid type of woman, for the mere reason that he is completely dominated not by a woman, but by women. His whole being is absorbed in women.

He is obsessed by the very thought of women. He is the man who will attempt familiarity with every woman he meets, who will stop his automobile at corners to invite in any woman who happens to be there.

The shame and the sorrow and the unhappiness caused the woman who marries a phallic type of man, or the man who is tied to a clitorid woman, need hardly be dwelt upon.

How to prevent the mating of an orchitic man with a clitorid woman, or that of a uterine woman with a phallic man?

It is a question that no one at present is able to answer. With the research work carried out in psychology and sexology we will in time learn how to tell a phallic man and a clitorid woman before marriage.

[Maurice Chideckel, M.D., *The Single, the Engaged, and the Married* (1936).]

IF YOU'RE IN THE MARKET FOR A BRIDE, YOU'LL WANT TO USE THIS VALUABLE SHOPPING LIST

You are thinking of matrimony. You would, of course, like to be sensible in your choice. Consider the following suggestions:

Do not select a woman with a temperament very similar to your own. You may judge of temperament by the color of the hair and skin, by the shape of the body and intensity of the nervous system.

Do not select a woman with a forehead shaped like your own.

If you are large, do not marry a small woman. The disparity in size should not be great. The several reasons for this advice are too obvious to need mention.

Such an error among animals often proves fatal, as indeed it often does among human beings.

Avoid a small waist as you would the plague.

73

If you join your fortunes to those of a pale, nervous, cold-blooded, fainting creature, you will spend the rest of your life bemoaning your folly.

Do not select an over-dressed woman. Excess of jewelry and other ornament shows a weakness, not to say vice, intolerable in your nearest friend and companion. It is vulgar and cheap, and is never found in superior persons.

Shun the untidy as you would an open drain.

Give an unloving daughter a wide berth.

Avoid ignorant girls and those with excessive accomplishments. If in this country a young woman is exceptionally ignorant, it proves a lack of capacity, while an excess of accomplishments shows a certain light-headedness, a certain lack of the plain, substantial qualities which are so desirable in a life-long companion.

Avoid very homely and very handsome women. If your choice is very ugly, she will constantly wound your taste in herself and in your children; and if she is very beautiful, all the men in the neighborhood will be likely to find it out, and some of them may tell her about it, or she may chance to look in the glass and discover it herself.

Don't marry your cousin.

Your wife should be over twenty years of age.

[Lewis, *Chastity.*]

IT HAS BEEN SAID THAT DIRTY OLD MEN
NEED LOVE TOO. MANY OF THEM
HAVE NO TROUBLE FINDING IT

It is inconceivable with what stupid and ridiculous vanity lecherous old men are wont to seek for young wives.

It is still more inconceivable that their search is so often successful.

The fact is usually attributable to the cupidity of parents, who do not hesitate to sacrifice their daughters to the interests of position or fortune.

In these monstrous alliances, whether we consider the reciprocal situation of the parties thus abusively joined, or the kind of progeny which is likely to result from them, we are equally moved with disgust and compassion.

We shall not review the dangers which we have already sufficiently exposed, inherent to the exercise of the genital sense in advanced age.

It is true that these dangers are only for the man, but they are so much the more imminent, as the young wife is more capable of arousing the sensual appetite by her graces, her youth, and all those other attractions with which she is endowed.

Alas! for the old dotard who dares to think of this enchanted cup!

Nature will assuredly avenge herself most cruelly for her violated laws.

"It is better to be an old man's darling than a young man's slave" is a proverb which reveals the corruption of our manners and the stupid infamy which makes of the nuptial couch an arena of debauch as detestable as the very slums of vice.

The interests of posterity, no less than of public morals, demand prohibitory laws upon this subject, and we call upon our legislators to boldly prescribe the extreme difference in age, beyond which it shall be unlawful for marriages to be solemnized.

[A Physician, *Satan.*]

THE PROPER AGE FOR MARRIAGE; OR, HE AND SHE—HOW OLD SHOULD THEY BE?

In no case should the age of the woman exceed that of her husband, to however slight an extent.

The earlier relative period of "old age" will mark this disparity very painfully as time progresses, a disparity which must gradually develop itself in the decade of thirty to forty.

So, while the husband appears in the prime of his manhood,

"the sere, the yellow leaf" is too obviously stealing over the wife.

There is something exceedingly touching in the efforts put forth by these forlorn wives to hide the inexorable ravages of time.

But the resources of art, albeit dangerous to health, cannot long postpone the evil day when the poor creature, the senior of her husband, finds herself the unmistakable "old woman," no longer personally attractive to her husband, himself, perhaps in the very pride of manly beauty.

It is in precisely these circumstances that so many men justify themselves in the establishment of criminal relations, often introducing their paramours into the very household, under the guise of servants, governesses, etc., but more frequently maintaining separate establishments.

These horrors are too often known or suspected by the unhappy wife, who, "for the sake of peace," or "to avoid publicity," or "on account of the children," or from womanly pride, and, in many cases, from pure Christian fortitude, endures her torture in silence.

The age properly considered "marriageable," is a question of which there can be no absolute solution.

As a general rule, it is imperative that the full growth shall have been attained, the vital organs in good condition, and those of generation free from all faulty conformation which may interfere with the consummation of the marriage.

It is also essential that in man the sexual instinct shall have become sufficiently awakened, that the desire for sexual relations shall have created in some sort a necessity.*

In a word, both sexes should have reached the age of procreative maturity. This period is distingusihed from that of puberty by the term *nubility;* that is, the age suitable for marriage.

Extended observation would lead us to recommend strongly a difference of from five years as the minimum to fifteen years as the maximum should be regarded in the choice of companions, as there is fully that difference in the two sexes in "growing old."

In our temperate climate, we would indicate twenty-one as the nubile age of women, and twenty-six as that of men.

*A caution but little required in this age and country.

[A Physician, *Satan.*]

YOUNG WOMEN MUST CONSTANTLY BE ON THE ALERT THAT THEIR INTENDED IS NOT A VICTIM OF THE BAD TRIO

You are more than twenty years of age; you are thinking of matrimony. I submit for your consideration the following advice:

As you would shun shipwreck, shun the victims of tobacco, alcohol and lust. These evils constitute the BAD TRIO.

They are rarely separated. You may hardly credit the following statements; yet they are true:

Of one hundred men who use tobacco, ninety-five use strong drink, — it may be privately, and in "moderate" quantities.

Of one hundred men who use strong drink, more than ninety-five use tobacco.

Of one hundred who use these poisons, every one of them has excited amativeness, and a very large proportion of them indulge it more or less outside the bars.

Can anything be more pitiful than a sweet, pure girl led to the altar, like a lamb to the slaughter, by a slave of the Bad Trio? This life presents few sadder scenes. Does it differ much from the brutal slave dealer leading the pretty quadroon from the auction-block to his plantation? There is a difference: the bride consents.

I will not advise you to avoid the sons of those who have served in the ranks of the Bad Trio, but you certainly run a great risk in marrying the offspring of a sot.

He may not turn out a drunkard, but he has certainly received an imperfect brain. No inebriate can give his child a well-poised moral nature.

Avoid a dandy. He is a poor, weak post to tie to, but not quite so unreliable as a lazy shiftless fellow. Better drown yourself than marry this kind of chap.

A man with great love of money, niggardly in all his expenditures, a close-fisted, miserly man, is more to be dreaded than the spendthrift. The miser may be a producer, thus in the long run, perhaps a better *citizen* than the spendthrift, but to the wife a miserly husband is a great affliction. What can be more exasperating than, when in plain sight of thousands she asks for a hundred, to hear, in sharp tones, "Where's the dollar I gave you last week?"

If you are bright, you will not be long in finding out whether your suitor loves you for your body only. If his approaches show this to be the sort of love he bears you, you are an idiot to consent to become his wife.

Before the first year is over he will love some other human female. And then you will have plenty of time during his absence to cry over your miserable weakness in selling your person for board and clothes.

If you are a clean woman, I need not advise you to shun a fellow with dirty linen and hands. He would prove an unceasing affliction.

And finally, I scarcely need advise one with womanly instincts not to hold her personal charms cheap even after marriage. Up to the hour of the ceremony you have remained intact. Nothing will contribute so much to the preservation of your husband's devotion as great reserve and modesty on your part.

A separate bed is priceless.

[Lewis, *Chastity*, pp. 229-31.]

A WARNING TO ANY MAN FOOLISH ENOUGH TO THINK ABOUT MARRYING A CALIFORNIA WOMAN

The importance of a man marrying younger than himself is obvious.

Women age much faster than men. The nervous system is frailer, and the metabolic mechanism of the entire body far more sensitive and delicate. Their charm, and therefore the sexual life, are shorter in duration.

In California, Mr. Powers tells us, women are handsome in their carefree, untoiling youth, but break down after twenty-five to thirty, and become, many of them, positively ugly.

[J. Richardson Parke, Sc.B., Ph.G., M.D. (former acting assistant surgeon, U.S. army), *Human Sexuality*—A Medico-Literary Treatise of the Laws, Anomalies, and Relations of Sex, with Especial Reference to Contrary Sexual Desire (Philadelphia: Professional Publishing, 1906), p. 133.]

WHY MOST YOUNG AMERICAN WOMEN ARE NOT FIT TO TAKE THEIR PLACE IN A REPUBLICAN HOME

(From Rev. A.D. Mayo's "Essay on Woman in America")

The crowd of American girls do what women would do everywhere; neglect the higher culture of the soul in scheming or waiting for the sensual advantages of life, and spend the first quarter of a century rather in superficial occupations and inquiring after desirable husbands than in toiling to become good wives and republican mothers.

This fearful push for the material prizes of our National life, explains the imperfect education of American young women. Mothers and daughters vie in the cultivation of those temporary graces and accomplishments which are supposed to bring young men to a crisis in the affections, while the solid qualities which can alone retain the love of a rational man or fit a woman for genuine success, and postponed till life is upon them.

. . . And this is the secret cause of the fearful collapse of female health in America; for standing on tiptoe and watching a chance to leap on board a fairy's floating palace that wavers over a stormy sea, is not a healthy, though an exciting occupation. It forces children through the grades of girlhood with steam-power rapidity to young ladyhood, while they should be romping in pantalets, learning science or household duties under their teachers or mothers. The rush of energy to the surface of life, the excitements, hopes and fears of a young lady's career, leave the deep places of the heart dry, and create a morbid restlessness of the affections that preys upon the very springs of physical existence.

79

So the majority of American girls, when they have obtained their lover, are not physically fit to become his wife and the mother of his children ...

The republican home that shall cheer, console, and elevate the American people, and the republican society that is but its extension and idealization, are yet a vision.

[A Physician, *Satan.*]

MEN WANT WOMEN WHO HAVE THAT ONE VERY SPECIAL TALENT

A man wants a wife who will make something of him, whose influence will ever inspire him to do his best.

What kind of a woman should she be?

For one thing, a man does not want a mere toy wife, something too fine, too ethereal for real use.

She should be a woman who can bear her share of all the burdens, who can endure toil and sacrifice, and grow all the lovelier meanwhile.

Again, the wife a man chooses should be a good housekeeper. To some romantic young lovers this will seem a very prosaic feature to put into the picture, But never mind: they will not be very many weeks married before they will come down out of the clouds to walk on common earth and then, alas! If the poor woman does not prove a good housewife!

There are women who live in sentimental dreams, neglecting meanwhile the duties that lie close to their hands. Good breakfasts, dinners and suppers, good bread, good coffee — in a word, good housekeeping. Far more than any young lovers dream does wedded happiness depend upon just such unromantic things as these.

[Shannon, *Nature's Secrets.*]

AFTER THE MARRIAGE

The Kind of Preparation for Marriage given by the Parents of
the past generations

NO WEDDING NIGHT IS COMPLETE WITHOUT SOME ORAL ACTIVITY. TRY THIS:

When the ceremony is over and you have retired to your chamber, make a little speech to your wife. The following will do:

MY PRECIOUS COMPANION: During our courtship we have been very happy. It has been the

CONTINUE YOUR COURTSHIP

supreme joy of my life. We both feel that in possessing each other we have secured our greatest good. The instinct which underlies this love between husband and wife would quickly disappear if we gave ourselves up to the unrestrained indulgence of passion. As we prize this precious love, we must not only avoid excess, but we must preserve our delicacy and modesty.

[Lewis, *Chastity.*]

HOW TO BE A GREAT WIFE

Love Him — A wife loves as naturally as the sun shines. Love is your best weapon. You conquered him with that in the first place. You can reconquer by the same means.

DO NOT CONCEAL YOUR LOVE *for* HIM

Do Not Conceal Your Love from Him—If he is too crowded with care, and too busy to seem to heed your love, you need to give all the greater attention to securing his knowledge of your love.

If you intermit he will settle down into a hard, cold life with increased rapidity. Your example will keep the light on his conviction. The more he neglects the fire on the hearth, the more carefully must you feed and guard it. It must not be allowed to go out.

Once out you must sit ever in darkness and in the cold.

Cultivate the Modesty and Delicacy of Your Youth—The relations and familiarity of wedded life may seem to tone down the sensitive and retiring instincts of girlhood, but nothing can compensate for the loss of these.

However much men admire the public performance of gifted women, they do not desire boldness and dash in a wife. The blush of a maiden's modesty is more powerful in hallowing and governing a home than the heaviest armament that ever a warrior bore.

Cultivate Personal Attractiveness—This means the stor-

CULTIVATE PERSONAL
ATTRACTIVENESS

ing of your mind with a knowledge of passing events, and with a good idea of the world's general advance.

If you read nothing, and make no effort to make yourself attractive, you will soon sink into a dull hack of stupidity.

Study Your Husband's Character—He has his peculiarities. He has no right to many of them but you can avoid many hours of friction.

The good pilot steers around the sunken rocks that lie in the channel. The engineer may remove them, not the pilot. You are more pilot than engineer. Consult his tastes. It is more important to your home that you should please him than anybody else.

Practice Economy—Many families are cast out of peace into discord by being compelled to fight against poverty. When there are no great distresses to be endured or accounted for, complaint and fault-finding are not so often evoked.

Keep your husband free from the annoyance of disappointed creditors, and he will be more apt to keep from annoying you.

To toil hard for bread, to fight the wolf from the door, to resist impatient creditors, to struggle against complaining pride at home, is too much to ask of one man.

A crust that is your own is a feast, while a feast that is purloined from unwilling creditors is a famine.

[Jefferis and Nichols, *Safe Counsel.*]

EXPLAINING *the* NEED *of a* NEW HAT

NEVER HAVE SEX
AFTER A FULL MEAL

Copulation is slow and dangerous immediately after a meal and during the two and three hours which the first digestion needs, or having finished a rapid walk or any other violent exercise. In the same way, if the mental faculties are excited by some mental effort, by a theatre party or a dance, rest is necessary, and it is advisable to defer amatory experience till the next morning.

[Talmey, *Love.*]

ONE THING THAT WILL TURN OFF A
HIGHLY CULTURED HUSBAND

One of the author's patients, a young woman of twenty-two, mother of one child, was sexually so excited during menstruation that her husband asked for a remedy to appease his wife's excitement who demanded frequent intercourse during menstruation.

Coitus during this period had an unaesthetic effect upon the highly cultured husband.

[Talmey, *Love.*]

SEX CAN BE ELECTRIFYING: OR
THE PURPOSE OF PUBIC HAIR

In order that this mingling of the male and female sources of life may be possible, it is necessary that there be a union of the male and female generative organs.

87

For such a meeting, the penis is filled with blood, all its blood vessels being distended to their utmost capacity, till the organ becomes stout and hard, and several times its dormant size, as has already been told. In this condition it is able to penetrate, to its utmost depths, the vaginal passage of the female, which is of a nature to perfectly contain the male organ in this enlarged and rigid condition. Under such conditions, the penis is inserted into the widened and distended vaginal passage.

Once together, a mutual back and forth, or partly in and out movement of the organs is begun and carried on by the man and woman, which action further enlarges the parts and raises them to a still higher degree of tension and excitement.

It is supposed by some that this frictional movement of the parts develops an electrical current, which increases in tension as the act is continued; and that it is the mission of the pubic hair, which is a non-conductor, to confine these currents to the parts in contact.

[H. W. Long, M.D., *Sane Sex Life and Sane Sex Living* — Some Things That All Sane People Ought to Know about Sex Nature and Sex Functioning; Its Place in the Economy of Life, Its Proper Training and Righteous Exercise (New York: Eugenics, 1919), pp. 49-50.]

SIX WAYS TO DO IT— AND YOU THOUGHT THERE WAS ONLY ONE!

The positions for copulation are six in number as used by different races at different epochs. They are

Man above
Man below
Standing
Sitting
Lateral, or side by side
From the rear

[Talmey, *Love*, p. 44.]

COLD WOMEN SHOULD SHOW WARMTH TOWARD HOT HUSBANDS— EVEN IF THEY'VE JUST HAD THEIR HAIR DONE OR HAVE A HEADACHE OR ARE TOO TIRED—AGAIN

Too many women regard the sexual act as a nuisance, as an ordeal, as something disagreeable to get through with as quickly as possible.

One great cause is congenital frigidity.

The woman is cold, frigid, has no desire for sex relations and experiences no pleasure, no sensation from them.

Such women are not to blame; they are to be pitied. But even they can behave so as not to repel their husbands.

And I would emphasize: Do not repel your husbands when they ask for sexual favors — at least do not repel them too often.

[William J. Robinson, M.D., *Sex Knowledge for Women and Girls* — What Every Woman and Girl Should Know (New York: Critic and Guide, 1917).]

THE "OTHER WOMAN"— WHY SHE ISN'T A NICE PERSON

To the terrifying menaces of the American Home must be added the "other woman."

Like an icy gust of wind she rushes in and chills the soul of father and husband. Under the blow stagger mother and children. She torpifies the senses of the most sensible man. She hushes the voice of conscience of a truly good man who, because of her, deserts his family without a pang.

No characterization precisely fits the other woman. Those whom the author observed were females of low cunning and of questionable moral integrity. They mastered the art of parading their sex, and engulfing men by that parade.

[Chideckel, Single, Engaged, Married.]

WILL HE NO' COME BACK AGAIN?

HOW MARRIAGE, SEX, AND PREGNANCY CAN HELP FAT LADIES

The tiresome inconvenience of being obliged to carry around everywhere from forty to a hundred pounds of useless, clogging fat, besides rendering its puffing victims short-breathed, creates the earnest inquiry, "How can it be lessened or obviated?"

1. By bearing as long and often as possible; because this promotes the legitimate consumption of this fat-producing material, as well as that womb-action which ejects it.

2. By eating lightly. Of course the more you eat, the more material must be stowed away in this form. Also avoid all fat meats, butter, and sweets, but eat freely of acid fruits, particularly lemons and lean meat, but not rich gravies.

3. By breathing deeply and copiously, so as to burn up as much of this carbon as possible by means of the lungs.

4. By keeping all the channels of evacuation open, the bowels and skin in particular, so as to cast out as much waste material as possible through all the other outlets. Squaw-vine tea will also aid in its diminution. Sleep sparingly.

5. But your greatest cure consists in promoting womb-action, since its great cause is its dormancy; for whatever increases sexual action and restoration will reduce this fat.

6. The true relief of extra fat girls consists in a right hearty love and marriage, along with maternity.

These prescriptions will certainly not hurt you, which is something, and in any event will do you only good. Try them, and "report progress."

[Fowler, *Sexual Science*, pp. 910-11.]

THE BRIDE.

EVEN THOUGH A MAN AND A WOMAN MAY SEEM MADE FOR EACH OTHER, CERTAIN IMPORTANT PARTS MAY BE POORLY MATCHED

It is a matter of misfortune, and yet one of not infrequent occurrence, that the sex organs of husband and wife are *not well matched;* and that trouble, sometimes of a most serious nature, results.

When this condition is found to exist, it should be treated sanely and wisely, and the chances are many to one that the difficulty can be overcome, to the full satisfaction of both parties concerned.

In such cases, the mis-matching usually arises from the fact that the penis of the husband is too long for the vagina of the wife. This is very apt to be the case where the wife is of the "dumpy" sort, with a small mouth and short fingers, while the husband is "gangling," large mouthed and long fingered.

These are facts that ought to be taken into account before and which should figure in determining whether the parties are "suited" to each other. They *would* be regarded in this way, too, if they were generally known, as they most surely are not.

[Long, *Sane Sex*, pp. 104-5.]

THE MECHANICS OF THE SEX ACT FULLY EXPLAINED!

The *modus operandi* of the sexual act itself is so well understood as to require little attention.

[Parke, *Sexuality.*]

THE MODEST WOMAN, LIKE A GOOD SOLDIER, DOES HER DUTY— BUT SHE NEVER VOLUNTEERS

Passion in Women — There are many females who never feel any sexual excitement whatever; others again, to a limited degree, are capable of experiencing it.

The best mothers, wives and managers of households know little or nothing of the sexual pleasure. Love of home, children and domestic duties are the only passions they feel.

As a rule, the modest woman submits to her husband, but only to please him; and, but for the desire of maternity, would far rather be relieved from his attentions.

[Shannon, *Nature's Secrets*, p. 162.]

THE AFFECTIONATE HUSBAND AND WIFE.

THE DANGER OF DOUBLE BEDS; OR,
IF YOU WANT GOOD HEALTH,
ALWAYS SLEEP WITH YOURSELF

It would be difficult to find two persons exactly equal in bodily powers. When sleeping together, between the same pair of sheets, the stronger will absorb vitality from the weaker. One person will arise refreshed for the day's work, the other more or less enervated.

When two persons occupying the same bed are husband and wife, in addition to the depletion of one's vitality, there is the temptation to amorous excess, which is avoided by seperate beds.

Of this Dr. Ruddock says: "Married persons should adopt more generally the rule of sleeping in separate rooms, or at least in separate beds, as is almost the universal custom in Germany and Holland.

"Opportunity makes importunity."

[Greer, *Wholesome Woman.*]

SEX CAN SEEM CRUEL. IN FACT, SOME
WOMEN ACT AS IF THEY ARE
COUNTESS DRACULA

Moraglia claims that some women's features manifest cruelty during conjugation.

At the beginning of the orgasm the face becomes distorted, and by showing her teeth such a woman assumes a certain ferocity of expression that is sometimes frightening.

One of the author's patients, a woman of twenty-six years of age, mother of two children, would take on a cruel look at the heights of her sexual excitement immediately before the orgasm.

This frightened the husband so that he sought medical advice.

She would also grab her consort's lips and tongue with her teeth and bite them.

Slight sadistic features are, therefore, not uncommon in women. Especially in modern times, with the increasing effemination *(sic)* of men and the corresponding masculination *(sic)* of women, the aggressive woman is not so great a rarity.

The biting and scratching of the companion during sexual excitement is, therefore, not uncommon and falls within physiological limits.

But when the individual is driven to whip, pinch and prick the body, or particularly, the genitals of her companion in the blind impulse to satisfy sexual desire, such expression of gratification does not correspond with the natural purposes, and the acts become perverse.

[Talmey, *Love*, p. 33.]

A GOOD WOMAN WILL TAKE AN ADULT VIEWPOINT TOWARD HER HUSBAND'S ADULTERY

We, advanced sexologists, know that not all men, no more than all women, are made in the same mould, and what is possible or even easy for nine may be very difficult or absolutely impossible for the tenth.

We know that there are some men to whom an iron-clad monogamic relation is absolute impossibility. The stimulation of other woman — either purely mental, spiritual stimulation or the stimulation of physical relations — is to them like breath in the nostrils.

In fact, there are some men whose very possibility of loving their wives depends upon this freedom of association with other women. They can be extremely kind to and love their wives tenderly, if they can at the same time associate — spiritually or physically — with other women. If they are entirely cut off from any association with any other woman they begin to feel irritable, bored, may become ill, and their feeling towards their wives may become one of resentment, ill-will, or even one of hatred. This is not the place to talk of the wickedness of such men — thus they are made and with this fact we have to deal.

What is the wife of such a man to do?

Two lines of conduct are open to her — two avenues of exit. The line of conduct will depend upon her temper and upon her ideas of sexual morality. But she ought to select the line of conduct which will cause the least pain, the least unhappiness.

CAN IT BE HE IS UNTRUE?

If she is a woman of a proud, independent temper, particularly if she belongs to the militant type, she will leave her husband in a huff, regardless of consequences.

But if she is a woman of the gentler, more pliable, more supple (and I may also say more subtle) type, and if she really loves her husband, she will overlook his little foibles, peccadilloes and transgressions — and she may live quite happily.

And the time will come when the husband himself will give up

97

his peccadilloes and transgressions and will cleave powerfully to his wife, will be bound to her by bonds never to be torn asunder. *I know of several such cases.*

And I will take this opportunity to say that I have the deepest contempt for the wife who, on finding out that her husband had committed a transgression or that he has a love affair, leaves him in a huff, or makes a public scandal, or sues for divorce. Such a wife *never* loved her husband, and he is well rid of her. And what I said about the wife applies with *almost* equal force to the husband.

[Robinson, *Woman*, pp. 397-99.]

THE FREQUENCY OF COPULATION: BENJAMIN FRANKLIN SET A GOOD EXAMPLE FOR US ALL

We are now led to anticipate the question, "How frequently does health or prudence permit the repetition of the marital act?"

No positive rule can be stated on this subject, dependent, as it is, on so great a variety of conditions, as individual temperaments, state of health at the moment, etc., but general principles can be clearly stated, from which may be readily deduced rules for particular instances.

Regard must always be had to instructions already stated; namely that nothing should induce a man to gratify his own desires at the expense of his wife's comfort or inclination; that the lawful pleasures of wedlock should never be permitted to degenerate into mere animal lust; that the rule should be, in all cases, too keep within but never to exceed the limits of fond desire.

Franklin's rule for eating, always to rise from the table with an appetite for more, can wisely be applied to the conjugal act — never repeat it so frequently but that the ability on both sides exists for further indulgence.

Perhaps most men learn this lesson soon enough for themselves, but a strongly passionate woman may well-nigh ruin a man of feebler sexual organization than her own, and so it is important that the woman also should be familiarized with the "physiology of matrimony," sufficiently, at least, to refrain from too exacting or frequent demands.

From once to thrice a month may be stated as a fair average frequency for the indulgence during the comparative youth and health of both parties.

["Satan In Society" by a Physician (Nicholas Francis Cooke) 1876]

GIVE YOUR SEXUAL APPARATUS A WELL-DESERVED VACATION. TEN DAYS OUGHT TO DO IT

Expressed in general terms (which, of course, will not fit everybody) my view may be formulated thus: The mutually best regulation of intercourse in marriage is to have three or four days of repeated unions, followed by about ten days without any unions at all, unless some strong external stimulus has stirred a mutual desire.

[Dr. Marie Carmichael Stopes, *Married Love* (New York: Eugenics, 1918, 1927, 1931), p. 61.]

THERE IS ONLY ONE GOOD REASON FOR SEXUAL RELATIONS

If it is noble and beautiful for the betrothed lover to respect the law of marriage in the midst of the glories of courtship, it may even be more noble and beautiful for the wedded lover to respect the unwritten laws of health and propagation in the midst of the ecstasies of sexual union.

Exchange of magnetic elements rebuilds waning vitality;

while the full procreation act, which ends with ejaculation of the seminal fluid, and a nervous spasm on the part of both participants, offers no compensation to either, except gratification of the animal impulse. It is only right when children are desired.

[Greer, *Wholesome Woman.*]

SOME HARSH WORDS FOR THOSE WHO STILL CLING TO THE "PHYSICAL NECESSITY" THEORY AS AN EXCUSE FOR COPIOUS COITUS

Adelaide Proctor in a little poem says that

A loving woman find heaven or hell
On the day she is made a bride.

This is not unchangeably true. It has often occurred when an innocent, ignorant girl, negatively pure, has been married to a man of habits positively evil. Trained to the belief that intimacy is impure, she may be shocked and horrified to be embraced by a

FIRST FIVE YEARS OF MARRIAGE.   FIVE YEARS LATER.

100

man who approaches her without a sense of delicacy; and thus she may find "hell."

Women sometimes sell themselves, or by their parents are sold into a state of dependence and sexual subjection, the consideration being a home, or a name and respectability, or money, or the belief that the subjection will be rewarded in the world to come.

Both husband and wife often believe in the "physical necessity" theory on his part.

You can almost select them from among your friends from their personal appearance and from the brood of children that spring from such a parental source.

He is coarse and dominating, she wan and faded and pathetic, the children cringing or unruly; the family anything but realizing that the strength of the nation depends on the integrity of home.

[Greer, *Wholesome Woman.*]

SOME HUSBANDS PREFER FRIGID WIVES, BUT MOST FRIGID WOMEN SHOULD TRY TO GIVE AN OSCAR-WINNING PERFORMANCE

Advice to Frigid Women, Particularly Wives — I wish to give you a piece of advice which is of extremely great importance to you.

I hesitated somewhat before writing this chapter, but the welfare of so many women depends upon following this advice, and I have seen the lives of so many wives spoiled on account of not having followed it, that I decided to devote a few words to the subject.

As you know, about one-third or one-quarter of all women (in other words, one out of every three or four) are sexually frigid.

They either have little or no sexual desire, or if they do have, they experience no voluptuous sensation during the act, and never have an orgasm.

101

If you are unmarried, well and good. But if you are married and happen to belong to the frigid type, then *don't inform your husband of the fact.*

It may lead to great and permanent trouble. Some husbands don't care. Some are even glad if their wives are frigid. They can then consult their own wishes in the matter, they can have intercourse whenever they want and *the way they want.*

They do not have to accommodate themselves to their wives' ways, they do not have to prolong the act until she gets the orgasm, etc.

In short, some husbands consider a frigid wife a God-sent treasure.

But, as I mentioned several times before, in sexual matters every man is a law unto himself, and some men feel extremely bad and displeased when they find out that their wives have "no feeling."

Some become furious, some become disgusted. Some lose all pleasure in intercourse, and some claim to be unable to have intercourse with any woman who is not properly responsive. Some begin to go to other women, while some threaten or demand a divorce (of course, such men cannot really love their wives; they may use their wives' frigidity as an *excuse* to get rid of them).

Now, a man has no way of knowing whether a woman has a feeling during the act or not, whether or no she enjoys it, whether or no she has an orgasm. These are subjective feelings, and the man cannot know unless you tell them.

If you belong to the independent kind, if you scorn simulation and deceit, if, as the price of being perfectly truthful, you are willing if necessary to part with your husband or give him a divorce, well and good.

You are a free human being, and nobody has a right to tell you what to do with your body.

But if you care for your husband, if you care for your home and perhaps children, and do not want any disruption, then the only thing for you to do is not to apprise your husband of your frigid condition.

And it won't hurt you to simulate a feeling which you do not experience, and even to imitate the orgasm. He won't be any the wiser, he will enjoy you more and nobody will be injured by your little deception, which is after all a species of white lie, and is nobody's business but your own. An innocent deception which hurts nobody, but, on the contrary, benefits all concerned, is perfectly permissible.

Some women are afraid to simulate a voluptuous or orgiastic feeling, because they think the husband can discover whether their feeling is genuine or they are only simulating. (Women, and men too, have funny ideas on sexual subjects).

This is not so. A notorious demi-mondaine, who was greatly sought because she was known to be so "passionate," confessed that not once in her life did she enjoy intercourse or experience an orgasm. But her mother, who also suffered with absolute frigidity, taught her to simulate passion, telling her that in that way she could make barrels of money: which she did.

It is deplorable that wives—or husbands—should ever be obliged to have recourse to deception or simulation; perfect frankness should be the ideal to be striven after.

But under our present social conditions and with the present moral code, an occasional white lie is the lesser of two evils; it may be the least of a dozen evils.

[Robinson, *Woman*, pp. 304-7.]

MIDDLE-AGED HUSBANDS WHO PRACTICE EXCESSIVE EJACULATION MAY BE HEADING FOR PREMATURE BURIAL

As age advances, new laws gain the ascendency in the married life.

In well-regulated lives, the sexual passions become less and less imperious, diminishing gradually, until at an average age of forty-five in the woman, and fifty-five in the man, they are but rarely awakened and seldom solicited.

After the "change of life" with woman, sexual congress while permissible, should be infrequent, no less for her sake than that of the husband, whose advancing years should warn him of the medical maxim: "Each time that he delivers himself to this indulgence, he casts a shovelful of earth upon his coffin."

[A Physician, *Satan.*]

SOCIAL
PLEASURES

A POX ON PERVERTED POSTCARDS!

Recreations Contribute to Immorality — The young people of today get their ideas from postcards, cheap shows, serial love stories and cheap novels.

One-third of the pictures exhibited at the cheap shows and plays at operas and theatres consists of every possible mode of spooning.

The billboards fairly blaze with pictures of enamored couples.

In nearly every assortment of postcards offered for sale by merchants can be found a large variety containing pictures of young men and women engaged in most suggestive positions.

Nine times out of ten the sensual artist makes the young man to appear innocent and passive and the young woman is made the aggressor. Suggestive sentences on the cards are usually from the lips of the young woman. Many of these pictures are secured by employing an attractive girl from the abodes of vice to pose with one of her male patrons.

Such postcards are insults to decent womanhood.

All good women should resent this.

[Shannon, *Personal Help*, p. 176.]

THOSE NASTY THINGS THEY SAY ABOUT
ACTRESSES ARE ALL TRUE

The modern stage is by no means a small factor in the development of sensuality.

No normal man, in the prime of life, can sit for hours and be entertained by semi-nude actresses, who engage in knee-dress dancing and other gymnastics, such as degrade their sex, and remain pure in his thoughts and habits.

These women are nearly all loose in their morals.

Some films exhibited in our five and ten-cent shows are quite as suggestive.

[Shannon, *Personal Help*, pp. 77-78.]

THERE IS TOO MUCH *SHOW* IN SHOW
BUSINESS

Some of the so-called best people in the profession are using the shimmy shake in song, dance and pantomime. Barefoot dancing with naked limbs being shown through transparent nets, abbreviated skirts with flesh- colored tights emphasizing the form and contour of the body by effective colored lights, are all part of the nefarious business which escapes ban under the guise of art.

The modern show appeals to the baser desire of the sexes. Even the advertising is full of nasty, dirty, ugly meaning. Posters of women partly in the nude, with boldly displayed titles such as "Twin Bed," "The Virgin Widow" and "French Frolics," are placed in every conceivable space where they will attract men, young and old.

[Jefferis and Nichols, *Safe Counsel*.]

SIGNS OF THE TIMES

108

THE LUSTFUL LIFE UPON THAT WICKED STAGE; OR, WOULD YOU WANT YOUR SON TO MARRY A GIRL WHO HAS APPEARED IN *SWAN LAKE?*

A woman who has no talent whatever as an actress, can, nevertheless, often cause a furore and draw large crowds to see her if she will strip herself of clothing to the extreme limits tolerated by law, and supply some sort of apology for such an appearance. The study of those so-called actresses seems to be constantly to devise something bolder and more indelicate than what any one else has brought out; and this way they attract large crowds of men and women, and receive enormous salaries from their managers.

Of course no real lady, if she were reflective, could think of allowing herself to be seen in such an assemblage where semi-nude women are openly degrading her sex, nor would a true gentleman attend places where he could not take the ladies of his family.

To such an extent do many actresses minister to the gratification of the sensual desires of the public, by the subtle art of suggestion, or by artistic lasciviousness, that the police have to keep a constant watch over the theatres in order to prevent the most flagrant indecencies.

At the World's Fair in Chicago all kinds of new sensual dances were introduced into the country from all parts of the world, the most familiar to the public being the "Danse du Ventre" and the "Kutchi-Kutchi."

Those who saw these performances could not fail to realize that they were beholding naked prostitutes, who were using every effort in their power to sexually excite the audience; and, to a lesser degree, the same can almost be said of the ballet-girls, who manage their limbs and their scanty drapery in ways which, to say the least, are impossible for pure womanhood.

These girls who perform in the ballet, or who otherwise appear in immodest parts, can be put down, not invariably, but almost without exception, as loose women.

Subjected to familiarity, course jests, and sensual admiration, and being as a matter of course both vain and poor, they fall easy victims to the debased profligates and fast young men who are so easily admitted to their acquaintance.

Both in Europe and America these so-called actresses—the chorus-girls and dancers—are classified *en masse* as loose women, and they are known by the medical profession to be more uniformly infected with venereal disease than are any other class of women. Nor can this be wondered at: Going from town to town, drinking and carousing with impure men and in rapid succession, elated by their association with so- called gentlemen who are above their station in life, they usually submit to the sexual embrace under the disadvantageous necessity of secrecy and without any attempt at hygienic precautions, and as a natural result they almost uniformly acquire venereal disease.

The modern stage is know to be a hotbed of impurity and divorce, and the actress who is not a divorcee or who has a clean reputation is the exception.

Olive Logan, herself an actress of note, whose father, mother, and five sisters were members of the theatrical profession, felt obliged to abandon the stage, and wrote: "I can advise no honorable, self-respecting woman to turn to the stage for support, with its demoralizing influences, which seem to be growing stronger and stronger day by day; where the greatest rewards are won by a set of brazen-faced, clog- dancing creatures, with dyed yellow hair and padded limbs, who have come here in droves from across the ocean."

Little improvement certainly has come about since her day.

[Scott, *Sexual Instinct*, pp. 158-60.]

IT IS HARD TO NAME A SOCIAL PLEASURE
THAT INFLAMES THE PASSIONS
AS HOTLY AS THE WALTZ

Whatever apologies may be offered for other forms of the dance as a means of exercise under certain restrictions, employed as a form of calisthenics, no such excuse can be framed in defense of "round dances," especially of the waltz.

In addition to the associated dissipation, late hours, fashionable dressing, midnight feasting, exposures through excessive exertions, improper dress, etc., it can be shown most clearly that dancing has a direct influence in stimulating the passions and providing unchaste desires, which too often lead to unchaste acts, and are in themselves violations of the requirements of strict morality, and productive of injury to both mind and body.

[Kellog, *Plain Facts.*]

IT IS ONLY A SHORT STEP FROM THE BALLROOM TO THE BEDROOM: WHY SHE SHOULD HAVE DANCED ALL NIGHT

Dancing and the Immodesties of Dress — In the ballroom many unappreciated influences are at work to excite the fancies, which may operate as visual, auditory, olfactory, or tactile impressions.

Except in childhood and old age — the neuter periods of life, when the *vita sexualis* is not largely influencing the thoughts and feelings — most men are naturally more or less excited by close approach to an attractive individual of the opposite sex, as are all animals; and this excitation is felt in greater intensity if the women dress so as to accentuate and bring into prominence her secondary sexual characteristics; and the various fetiches *(sic)* of dress and personal adornment exert even a stronger spell when the well-known physiological effects of perfumes and seductive music and superadded.

Young girls who have been modestly brought up have been known to cry bitterly from a sense of natural womanliness the first time they have been made to appear in ball dress; their pure instincts shrinking from showing the great expanse of bare

111

flesh, the dimple between the breasts, and the nude bosom and arms—for, upon their first appearance, they fully realize that they are indecently clad for the society of men.

In some of these ballrooms one may see upward of an acre of bare shoulders and bosom and arms, and it is impossible to doubt that many men are sexually inflamed in such an atmosphere.

The beautiful attribute of feminine modesty is at the best put to a severe strain in the ballroom, for the woman meet men, many of them impure, under circumstances which cannot bear analysis.

Women are largely to blame for apathetically permitting such improperly seductive attire to be worn, and for receiving and even welcoming into their circles men who are known to be unfit for introduction to young girls; in no surer way could they contribute to the humiliation of their own sex.

Of course dancing is fun! Who can resist the fascination of the enchanting music which compels the muscles to move in graceful cadence? Of course it must be intoxicatingly pleasurable to feel that one is so beautiful and so attractive to the men; and of course it is a treat for men to mix with women who should be at home in their boudoirs until more fittingly attired. But fun never excuses sin, nor can it be offered as a palliation for practices and customs which are scientifically known to be subversive of sexual control.

In the ballroom the girl feels secure because she knows that she is safe from the too-open demonstrations of her partner. Before others they can almost hug each other to music, place their arms round each other, and revel in the intoxicating fancies which are induced by the attractions of sex, of apparel, perfume, music, etc.

And, in addition, there is often a vivaciousness of irresponsibility with all this which is further courted at the punchbowl, and alcohol is known to have a far more erotic effect on women than on men.

If a list were made of the gentlemen's names at almost any large ball, many of them would be erased by a careful censor as unfit for association with decent women.

This is no mere matter of opinion, but an incontrovertible fact; and those are blind indeed who cannot see that the modern ball, with every feature in it sensuous and seductive, is what we call a secondary sexual love-feast, and that its present tendency is not in the direction of purity or a high civilization. It must be remembered that many of the men, and for that matter many of the women as well, are the descendants of ancestors who were lustful and perverse in their inclinations, and that such are congenitally vicious and abnormal in their sexual proclivities.

[Scott, *Sexual Instinct*, pp. 148-49, 154-57.]

FEW PEOPLE REALIZE HOW EXPLICIT TODAY'S POPULAR LITERATURE HAS BECOME. AN EXCERPT FROM A DIRTY BOOK

No other source contributes so much to sexual immorality as obscene literature.

When the devil determines to take charge of a young soul, he often employs a very ingenious method.

He slyly hands a little novel filled with "voluptuous forms," "reclining on bosoms," "languishing eyes," etc. I will give you a sample passage:

> Madly, wildly bent on possessing the lovely Helene, never for an instant does his glance wander from her face and form. With all the magnetism of fond affection firing his eyes, he stands waiting, gazing, and insisting — not in vain. In an ectasy of *abandon*, she rushes into his arms. He struggles to express in song his mad passion, and with her arms wound round about his neck, she listens, every action and look betokening the fervid, burning love that beats within her bosom, that deepens and darkens within her eyes, and lights his face like a fierce flame. Locked in each other's arms, the lovely pair, intent on each other, forget everything on earth below and in the heavens above . . . .

113

and so on for two hundred pages.

Publishing houses, the managers of which contrive to keep out of jail, send out tons of such stuff every month. Some of them affect respectability. I take the liberty to suggest a change in their business, one which I am sure would prove congenial, and would by comparison, serve the cause of virtue. Let them open a gambling-hell, or a house of prostitution. The moral level would be above their present trade, and the injury done the public would be as nothing in comparison.

Can you imagine a man born of woman, nursed and trained by maternal love, returning it all by devoting himself to the distribution of such filthy, deadly poison? None but God can measure the extent of the evil influence on these vile harpies. There are several wealthy publishers in this country whose business it is to run great steam engines and numberless machines in the preparation of this slime of the pit.

[Lewis, *Chastity.*]

BEFORE YOU SET FOOT ON THE DANCE FLOOR, MAKE SURE YOU HAVE A GOOD MAJOR-MEDICAL POLICY

The consequence of violent dancing may be really serious. Not only do delicate girls bring on, thereby, a violent palpitation of the heart, and their partners appear in a most disagreeable condition of solution, but dangerous falls ensure from it. I have known instances of a lady's head being laid open, a gentleman's foot being broken in such a fall, resulting, poor fellow, in lameness for life.

It is, perhaps, useless to recommend flat-foot waltzing in this country, where ladies allow themselves to be almost hugged by their partners, and where men must think it necessary to lift a lady almost off the ground, but I am persuaded that if it were introduced, the outcry against the impropriety of waltzing would soon cease. Nothing could be more delicate than the way a German holds his partner.

[Hartley, *Gentlemen's Etiquette.*]

A WOMAN HAS DIFFICULTY DOING ONE
THING WITH HER HANDS

The fact that women rarely applaud at the theatre or in the concert-room is no evidence that they do not appreciate a fine performance. To tell the truth, their hands are not well adapted for any great demonstration of their feelings; moreover, they have their gloves to consider. As for shouting "Encore!" or indulging in any other vocal manifestations of approval, such a proceeding would be regarded as highly indecorous. On the other hand, laughter and tears are easily induced, and these may be looked upon as legitimate outlets for their feelings.

[Leopold Wagner, *Manners, Customs, and Observances* (1894).]

CAUTION: YOUR CIGARETTE BOX MAY
BE DANGEROUS TO YOUR
MORALS

Modern ingenuity has made it possible to reproduce by engravings and chromo-lithographs thousands of pictures at a minimum cost; and as a result lewd illustrations are distributed everywhere, in the papers and magazines, in cigarette boxes, on the fences as theatrical posters, and, in fact, wherever they are likely to catch the public attention.

The employment of female models who are required to pose in the nude is a custom of the artist which is undoubtedly productive of much harm. If a physician were to needlessly expose a patient he would be severely condemned as unprofessional; but surely Art cannot be on such a lofty pedestal as to require the sacrifice of the modesty and self-respect of young girls who are reduced by necessity to offer up that part, at least, of their virtue.

115

No right-minded parent would allow a daughter to pose in scanty attire before any man, however pure—for it is well known that it is exceptional for these models to retain their virginity.

[Scott, *Sexual Instinct*, pp. 162-63.]

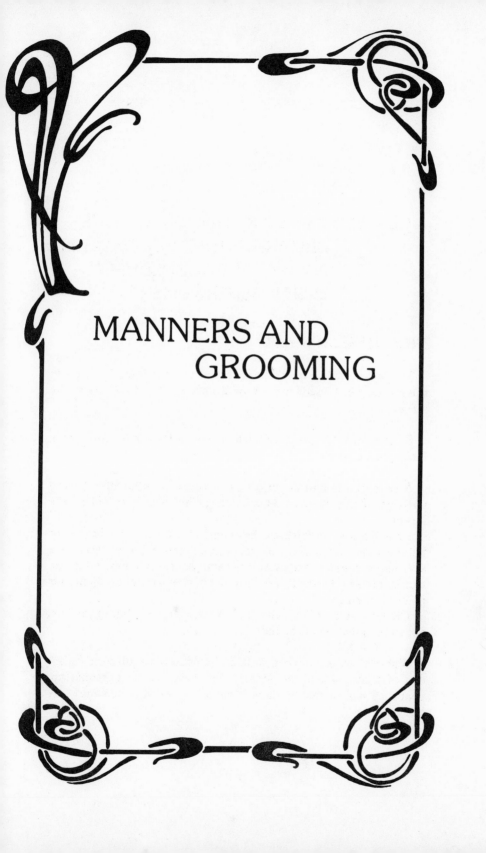

MANNERS AND
GROOMING

A GENTLEMAN NEVER STEPS ON A LADY'S DRESS OR PUTS BONBONS IN HIS POCKET, BUT HE DOES HELP IRISH WASHERWOMEN

Etiquette in the Street

You may bow to a lady who is seated at a window, if you are in the street; but you must not bow from a window to a lady in the street.

Be careful when walking with or near a lady, not to put your foot upon her dress.

A true gentleman never stops to consider what may be the position of any woman whom it is in his power to aid in the street.

He will assist an Irish washerwoman with her large basket or bundle over a crossing, or carry over the little charges of a distressed negro nurse, with the same gentle courtesy which he would extend toward the lady who was stepping from her private carriage.

The true spirit of chivalry makes the courtesy due to the sex, not to the position of the individual.

Where there are several ladies, and you are required to escort one of them, select the elderly, or those whose personal appearance will probably make them least likely to be sought by others.

You will probably be repaid by finding them very intelligent, and with a fund of conversation.

When driving a lady in a two-seated vehicle, you should assist her to enter the carriage, see that her dress is not in danger of touching the wheels, and that her shawl, parasol and fan are where she can reach them, before you take your own seat.

Etiquette for Calling

A call may be made upon ladies in the morning or afternoon; but in this country, where almost every man has some business to occupy his day, the evening is the best time for paying calls.
You will gain ground in easy intercourse and friendly acquaintance more rapidly in one evening, than in several morning calls.

Never make a call upon a lady before eleven o'clock in the morning, or after nine in the evening.

Never sit beside a lady upon a sofa, or on a chair very near her own, unless she invites you to do so.

Hints for Gentlemanly Deportment

Never enter a room, in which there are ladies, after smoking, until you have purified both *(sic)* your mouth, teeth, hair and clothes.
If you wish to smoke just before entering a saloon, wear an old coat and carefully brush your hair and teeth before resuming your own.
When you meet a lady at the head of a flight of stairs, do not wait for her to ascend, but bow, and go up before her.

Avoid the filthy habit of which foreigners in this country so justly complain — I mean spitting.

Table Etiquette

If in the leaves of your salad, or in a plate of fruit you find a worm or insect, pass your plate to the waiter, without any comment, and he will bring you another.

Never blow your soup if it is too hot, but wait until it cools. Never raise your plate to your lips, but eat with your spoon.

Never put fruit or bonbons in your pocket to carry them from the table.

When taking coffee, never pour it into your saucer, but let it cool in the cup, and drink from that.

If invited yourself to sing, and you feel sufficiently sure that you will give pleasure, comply immediately with the request.

If, however, you refuse, remain firm in your refusal, as to yield after once refusing is a breach of etiquette.

Traveling Etiquette

Never ridicule or blame any usage which seems to you ludicrous or wrong. You may wound those around you or you may anger them, and it cannot add to the pleasure of your visit to make yourself unpopular.

If in Germany they serve your meat upon marmalade, or your beef raw, or in Italy give you peas in their pods, or in France offer you frog's legs and horsesteaks, if you cannot eat the strange viands, make no remarks and repress every look or gesture of disgust.

Try to adapt your taste to the dishes, and if you find that impossible, remove those articles you cannot eat from your plate, and make your meal upon the others, but do this silently and quietly, endeavoring not to attract attention.

The best travelers are those who can eat cats in China, oil in Greenland, frogs in France, and macaroni in Italy; who can smoke a meerschaum in Germany, ride an elephant in India, shoot partridges in England, and wear a turban in Turkey.

[Hartley, *Gentlemen's Etiquette*, pp. 50-57, 180, 67-71, 78, 84, 203, 216.]

WOMEN WHO DO NOT WASH FOR SEVERAL YEARS ARE LIKELY TO REMAIN SINGLE

Perfect health is nearly as much dependent on pure sunlight as it is on pure air. A sunbath costs nothing, and that is a misfortune, for people are deluded with the idea that those things only can be good which cost money.

Ladies who have ample leisure and who lead methodological lives take a plunge or sponge bath three times a week, and a vapor or sunbath every day: The lady denudes herself, takes a seat near the window and takes in the warm rays of the sun. If, however, she be of a restless disposition, she may dance, instead of basking, in the sunlight.

Everybody cannot have beautiful hands, but there is no plausible reason for their being ill-kept.

Red hands may be overcome by soaking the feet in hot water as often as possible.

If the skin is hard and dry, use tar or oatmeal soap, saturate them with glycerine, and wear gloves in bed. Never bathe them in hot water, and wash no oftener than is necessary.

There are dozens of women with soft, white hands who do not put them in water once a month. The same treatment is not unfrequently applied to the face with the most successful results.

If such methods are used, it would be just as well to keep the knowledge of it from the gentlemen.

We know of one beautiful lady who has not washed her face for three years, yet it is always clean, rosy, sweet and kissable.

With some of her other secrets she gave it to her lover for safe keeping. Unfortunately, it proved to be her last gift to that gentleman, who declared in a subsequent note that "I cannot reconcile my heart and my manhood to a woman who can get along without washing her face."

[Mrs. E.C. Blakeslee, *Compendium of Cookery and Reliable Recipes* (1890).]

THE SECRET TO A SENSUOUS WOMAN'S SUCCESS IS OFTEN FOUND IN HER PANTIES

This may be considered too delicate or trifling a subject to discuss in an important sex book. But nothing is too delicate or too trifling that concerns human happiness, and you will believe me if I tell you that nice underwear or dainty lingerie plays a very important role in marital life.

And every married woman should have as fine and as dainty underwear as she can possibly afford. A fine or elaborate nightgown may be more important than an expensive skirt or hat.

Unfortunately, too many women ignore this fact. Externally they will be well dressed, while their petticoats, drawers and undershirts will be of the commonest quality and of questionable freshness and immaculateness. And if anything in a woman's toilet should be immaculately fresh and clean it is, I emphasize, her underwear.

Silk and lace and delicate batiste should be preferred, if they can be afforded, and attention should be paid to the color. As a rule, a delicate pink is the color that most men prefer.

The sex act with some men requires the most delicate adjustments, and the condition of the underwear may determine the man's desire and ability or inability to accomplish the act.

I therefore repeat: whether you are newly married or have been married a quarter of a century, be sure that your underwear is the very best that your means will allow you, and that it is always sweet, fresh and dainty. It will help you retain the affection of your husband.

[Robinson, *Woman*, pp. 345-46.]

SO YOUR KNIGHT IN SHINING ARMOR IS TURNING INTO A SLOB

Don't let your husband become a slob.
That is just what I mean. It is no use mincing words.

Some husbands have never acquired the habit—or if they have acquired it they quickly lost it—of regarding their wives as ladies.

"She is not a lady, she is only my wife," is a well-known joke, but some men think that before their wives they can be slovenly and unclean as they please.

Give your husband to understand that cleanliness and freshness is not a "sex-limited" attribute, and just as a husband wants his wife to be clean and dainty and well-groomed, so a wife may enjoy the same qualities in her husband.

Some women are very fastidious, and while they may say nothing to their husbands for fear of irritating them, they may think a good deal.

[Robinson, *Woman*, pp. 352-53.]

SINCE MEN ARE MORE ESTHETIC THAN WOMEN, A SMART WIFE AVOIDS SHOCKING A DELICATE HUSBAND

Some wives think that because they are married to their husbands they owe the latter no esthetic consideration.

Things that they would be horrified to let a stranger see they do before their husband's eyes without hesitation. For instance, not to beat around the bush, though the subject is not a pleasant one, they will urinate in their husband's presence, or they will let him see their soiled menstrual napkins, etc.

Some husbands may not mind it; but some men are very sensitive—men on the whole are more esthetic than women—and an indifference towards the wife may have its origin in some vulgar or unesthetic procedure on the wife's part.

The sexual act, as mentioned before, is a very delicate mechanism, and it is very easy to disarrange it. The fact of micturition before the man is known in many instances to have instantly abolished the man's sexual desire which was present before.

And a man told me that because he noticed in a closet a lot of rags soiled with menstrual blood he was unable to enjoy relations with his wife for several months.

You may think that these are small things, but life is made up of little things, and many a married life went smash on account of disregarding the little things.

[Robinson, *Woman*, pp. 346-47.]

HOW WOMEN CAN GOVERN, CONTROL, MANAGE, AND INFLUENCE MEN

Where is the woman would not be beautiful? If such there be — but no, she does not exist. From that memorable day when the Queen of Sheba made a formal call on the late lamented King Solomon until the recent advent of the Jersey Lily, the power of beauty has controlled the fate of dynasties and the lives of men.

How to be beautiful, and consequently, powerful, is a question of far greater importance to the feminine mind than predestination or any other abstract subject.

If women are to govern, control, manage, influence, and retain the adoration of husbands, fathers, brothers, lovers, or even cousins, they must look their prettiest at all times.

[Blakeslee, *Cookery.*]

PERFECT WOMANHOOD

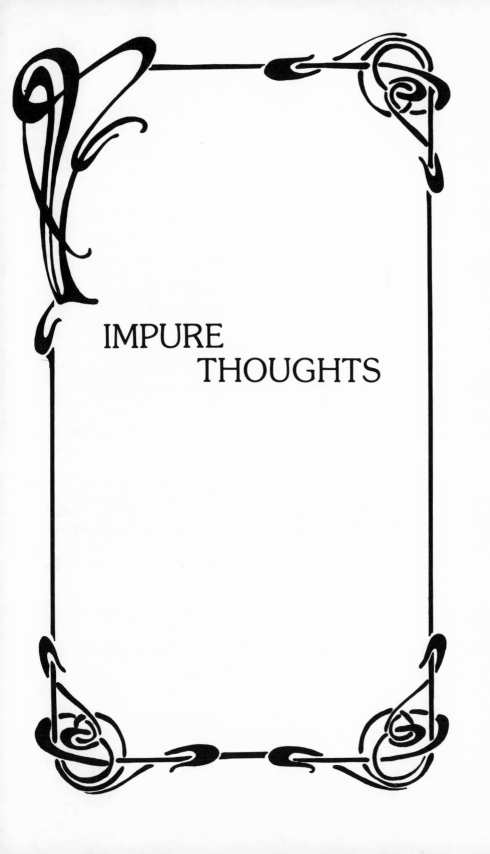

IMPURE
THOUGHTS

HOW ONE OLDER MARRIED WOMAN CAN
BE OF REAL SERVICE TO A DOZEN
SINGLE YOUNG MEN

When an intelligent young man comes to me for advice about sexual weakness, if his health and age be proper, I am in the habit of advising him to cultivate the intimate acquaintance of a pure woman, with reference to marriage.

Nothing ennobles manhood more surely than such associations.

And if for any good reason matrimony is out of the question, I still advise him to form a friendship with some true lady. It is best that she should be older than himself, a wife and a mother.

The wife of a manufacturer of my acquaintance has taken into pleasant intimacy a dozen or more of the young men employed by her husband, and one of them told me that a half-hour spent with her has driven out of his mind for days impure thoughts which were wont to harbor there.

One of the most potent safeguards against lust is an intimate association with pure women.

[Lewis, *Chastity*, p. 41.]

A MOTTO FOR YOUNG MEN TROUBLED BY
LEWD THOUGHTS

Remedy for Over-indulgence — If an unmarried man finds himself troubled with concupiscence, let him be more abstemious, and less stimulating and heating in his diet; let him take more active exercise in the open air; let him use the cold bath under proper conditions, and he will be greatly helped.

But that is not all.

He must have a proper chastity of mind; he must avoid lewd images and conceptions of his mind and imagination.

Let every young man's motto be: *The mind away from sexual thoughts, and the hands away from the parts.*

[Shannon, *Personal Help.*]

TEMPTED BY EROTIC FANCIES? TRY JOGGING—OR PLAYING WITH YOUR BEANBAG

Many people find it easier to banish erotic fancies by some occupation in which the body actively participates. To rise at once and attack a task requiring attention and care, with vigorous bodily movements, will instantly drive away all unclean thoughts.

Many have praised dumb-bells in this connection. I have known several to try bean-bags, practicing many games, throwing them up in a variety of ways, three, four, or five at a time.

But brisk walking, sawing wood, gardening, or any other exercise requiring attention and strong will, answers just as well.

Such efforts never fail.

[Lewis, *Chastity.*]

A MYSTERY SOLVED; OR, WHY IT'S HARD TO BE HAPPY WHEN YOU'RE HORNY

Where one person is injured by sexual commerce, many are made feverish and nervous by harboring lewd thoughts.

129

Rioting in visions of nude women may exhaust one as much as an excess in actual intercourse.

There are multitudes who would never spend the night with an abandoned female, but who rarely meet a young girl that their imaginations are not busy with her person. This species of indulgence is well-nigh universal; and as it is the source of all the other forms — the fountain from which the external vices spring, the nursery of masturbation and excessive coitus — I am surprised to find how little has been said about it. I have looked over many volumes upon sexual abuses, but do not recall a single earnest discussion of this point.

Believing that this incontinence of the imagination works more mischief than all other forms of the evil — that, indeed, it gives rise to all the rest — I am astounded that it has received so little attention.

The Venom Works Unsuspected. A Young man, of fine culture and morals, who for four years had filled a prominent pulpit, came to me with a derangement in his nervous system.

I immediately suspected that his peculiar symptoms had their origins in some abuse of the generative function; but knowing that a person of his character was not likely to be thus guilty, I inquired, somewhat reluctantly, if he had not suffered from nocturnal emissions.

He answered, "No, thank God, I have been preserved from all those wicked follies." I still sought for the clue, and said to him at length, "You will pardon me, but I cannot help suspecting that your difficulties are due to some sexual exhaustion."

He replied, "You are mistaken; I never practiced masturbation in my life; I have never had intercourse with a woman, and never but once had a nocturnal emission."

I asked, "Are you engaged?"

"Yes."

"How often do you see the object of your passion?"

"I spend every Thursday evening with her."

"You caress her?"

"Perhaps so."

"Is your mind occupied with sexual fancies?"

"It is, very much."

"Do you not feel worse on Friday than on any other day?"

"I do, and I have wondered that my visit to my friend, which is the happiest event of the week, should be followed by such a wretched day."

[Lewis, *Chastity*, pp. 26-27.]

130

DIRTY WORDS ARE A CURSE ON YOUR MOUTH

Use no profane language, utter no word that will cause the most virtuous to blush. Profanity is a mark of low breeding; and the tendency of using indecent and profane language is degrading to your minds.

Good men have been taken sick and become delirious. In these moments, they have used the most vile and indecent language. When informed of it, after a restoration to health, they had no idea of the pain they had given to their friends.

Think of this, ye who are tempted to use improper language and never let a vile word disgrace you.

[Hartley, *Gentlemen's Etiquette.*]

THE LINK BETWEEN SEX AND THE HEAD: HOW LUST CAN DRIVE YOU CRAZY

In his investigations of the asylums of one nation, Dr. Pique claims that he found that 82 per cent of all cases of insanity among females and 78 per cent among males, involved the sexual mechanism . . . and that early sex instruction would have wholly prevented many cases and would have postponed the mental breakdown in many cases until later in life.

[Shannon, *Natures Secrets*, p. 115.]

TOO MANY WEALTHY YOUNG WOMEN ARE LED ASTRAY BY BALLS AND SYMPHONIES

All medical authorities agree that nothing is more calculated to exalt sensibility, to sensualize the heart, and expose the nervous system to the most fatal perturbations than a luxurious and voluptuous education.

The reading of novels, the pleasures of the senses, the frequenting of balls and theatres, even the cultivation of accomplishments, such as music, dancing and the like, exerts a prodigious influence upon the female morale.

Says a famous author: "Daily experience proves that music especially saddens and enervates the mind, or immensely exalts the nervous system, and hence too often opens the door to all the vapors and nervous accidents which are the sad portion of women of the opulent classes."

[A Physician, *Satan.*]

MEN WHO HARBOR LEWD THOUGHTS LAUGH AT VICE AND SNEER AT PURITY AND THEY OFTEN BECOME EFFEMINATE

It is vain for a man to suppose himself chaste who allows his imagination to run riot amid scenes of amorous associations. The man whose lips delight in tales of licentiousness, whose eyes feast upon obscene pictures, who is ever ready to pervert the meaning of a harmless word or act into uncleanness, who finds delight in reading vivid portrayals of acts of lewdness — such a one is not a virtuous man.

Though he may never had committed an overt act of unchastity, if he cannot pass a handsome female on the street without, in imagination, approaching the secrets of her person, he is but one grade above the open libertine, and is as truly unchaste as the veriest debauchee.

O purity! How rare a virtue! How rare to find a face which shows no trace of sensuality!

One turns with sadness from the thought that human "forms divine" have sunk so low. The standard of virtue is trailing in the dust. Men laugh at vice and sneer at purity.

Foul thoughts, once allowed to enter the mind, stick like leprosy. They corrode, contaminate, and infect like the pestilence; naught but Almighty power can deliver from the bondage of concupiscence a soul once infected by this foul blight, this mortal contagion.

(Dr. Graham says;) "These lascivious daydreams and amorous reveries, in which young people, and especially the idle and the voluptuous and the sedentary and the nervous, are exceedingly apt to indulge, are often the source of general debility and effeminacy, disordered functions, premature disease, and even premature death, without the actual exercise of the genital organs!"

[Kellog, *Plain Facts.*]

DIRTY DREAMS LEAD TO DIRTY DEEDS

This perversion of a natural instinct, and these sudden lapses from virtue which startle a small portion of the community, and afford a filthy kind of pleasure to the other part, are but the outgrowths of mental unchastity.

"Filthy dreamers," before they are aware, become filthy in action. The thoughts mold the brain, as certainly as the brain molds the thoughts. Rapidly down the current of sensuality is swept the individual who yields his imagination to the contemplation of lascivious themes. Before he knows his danger, he finds himself deep in the mire of concupiscence. He may preserve a fair exterior; but the deception cannot cleanse the slime from his putrid soul.

How many a church member carries under a garb of piety a soul filled with abominations, no human scrutiny can tell.

How many pulpits are filled by "whited sepulchers," only the Judgement will disclose.

[Kellog, *Plain Facts.*]

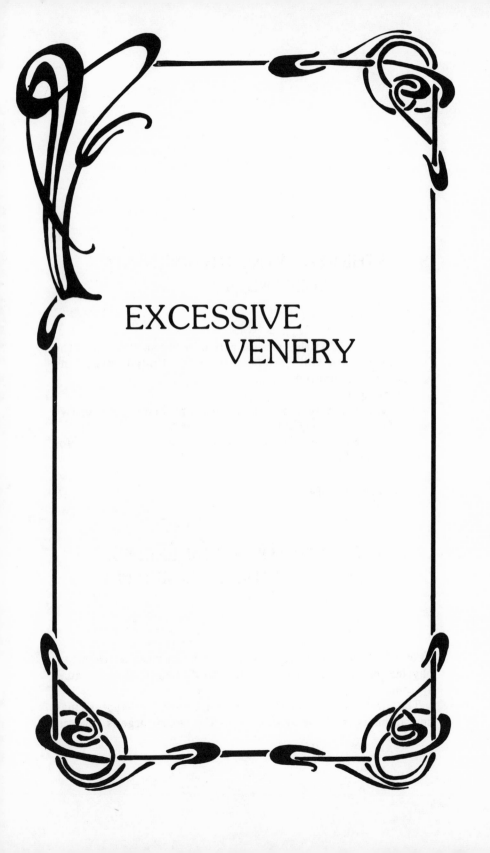

EXCESSIVE
VENERY

SEX IS THE REASON NORTH AMERICA IS GOING NUTS

"At the present rate of increase in insanity the last sane person will disappear from the United States and Canada in two hundred years."

'Startling, isn't it?

And yet this statement is from the published reports of two world-famous alienists within the last year.

Both agree that ignorance of the laws of sex is responsible for more cases of insanity than any other single factor.

[Jefferis and Nichols, *Safe Counsel.*]

ARE YOU A VICTIM OF SEXUAL EXCESS? CHECK THIS LIST FOR TELLTALE SYMPTOMS

Sexual Neurasthenia—By sexual neurasthenia we mean physical or mental exhaustion due to disorders of the sexual system.

The first as well as the most important cause of sexual neurasthenia is abuse or disease of the sexual organs such as

136

masturbation, excessive intercourse, excessive nocturnal emissions, withdrawal, lack of sexual satisfaction, spermatorrhea, or venereal infection.

Next in importance come those causes which for convenience may be classified under the term "mode of life," such as worry, overwork, suggestive literature, drama, or dress, bad companionship, and society's demand for a supression of sexual instinct.

And finally we cannot ignore the influence of heredity. It has been clearly shown that the offspring of neurasthenic parents are subject to the sexual disorders which bring on sexual neurasthenia.

Symptoms of Neurasthenia—In extreme cases of this disorder practically every organ in the body and its function is affected.

The following are usually present:

1. *Pains and aches in the back or over the kidneys.*

2. *Palpitation of the heart.*

3. *Poor circulation.*

4. *Frequent headaches.*

5. *Eyestrain.*

6. *Lack of ambition.*

7. *Inability to concentrate.*

8. *Melancholia.*

9. *Morbid fears.*

10. *Brain fag.*

11. *Extreme nervousness.*

12. *Sensitiveness.*

13. *Bashfulness.*

14. *Deranged appetite.*

15. *Digestive difficulties.*

16. *Impotence.*

17. *Shrunken or relaxed sex organs.*

18. Pollutions.

19. Lack of orgasm.

20. Masturbation.

21. Pains in the testicles.

22. Itching about the parts.

[Jefferis and Nichols, *Safe Counsel.*]

THE FREQUENT FORNICATOR WHO SOWS HIS WILD OATS SOON MEETS THE GRIM REAPER

It is a commonly expressed sentiment that "it is just as well for a man to sow his wild oats when he is young, for, if he does not, he may never get over the tendency, and perhaps sow them after marriage."

Nothing could be more pernicious than such a proposition; for a reformed profligate makes the poorest kind of a husband — often being corrupt in body, and perhaps having imperious mental concepts which we will call brain-stains.

Intercourse with different women is well known to morbidly increase desire, while married life bridles it and keeps passion under proper subjection.

The husband who has a clean record and a mind free from stain is far more apt to have perfect ease and perfect love for his wife; but indulgence in promiscuous fornication of course excludes the feeling of love, which is a physiological necessity in a true sexual relationship; and one who has been a fornicator is bound to have a soiled imagination, and perhaps a diseased body as well.

Through the association of ideas, trivial circumstances, as is well known, may produce impotency in men, so that they may have, in greater or lesser degree, a *horror femince* or loathing for all or for certain women; or perhaps they may be compelled to create stimuli ideally in order to be potent.

138

That this should be so is hardly to be wondered at when we consider that the sexual orgasm is attended with the most intense nerve excitement, and that the cerebral centers which preside over the emotions are in a state of intensified susceptibility during the act of copulation, so that the brain-cells, upon such occasions, are particularly liable to have permanent impressions firmly and ineradicably fixed upon them.

So intense is sexual excitement in some individuals that many of the frequent deaths of elderly men in bawdy-houses are attributed to syncope while in the sexual orgasm.

Male insects usually die after sexual congress; and some animals are so rapt in ecstasy during the act that they can be mutilated without their paying the slightest attention.

Even under the usual degree of intensity of excitement which is experienced during the consummation of the act, it is not to be wondered at that mental impressions which are then prominent become deep and lasting. Accordingly, if sentient men fornicate with the coarse, the low, the vicious, the strongly perfumed, and the voluptuously attired harlots, they may render themselves mentally soiled, and perhaps at a remote date be impotent for copulation with their pure wives, unless they resort to some sham or mental trickery.

[Scott, *Sexual Instinct.*]

ALWAYS BE SUSPICIOUS OF A MINISTER
WITH LARYNGITIS

The disease known as *clergyman's sore throat* is believed by many eminent physicians to have its chief origin in excessive venery. It is well known that sexual abuse is a very potent cause of throat disease.

[Kellog, *Plain Facts.*]

TOO MUCH SEX MAKES YOU GIDDY. IT ALSO HURTS YOUR BACK

Some of the most common effects of sexual excess are backache, lassitude, giddiness, dimness of sight, noises in the ears, numbness of the fingers and paralysis.

[Lewis, *Chastity.*]

THE U.S. ARMY KNOWS WHAT KEEPS YOUNG MEN HEALTHY

Sex is one of the most important things in your life, for it makes you a man. It's something to be proud of. But, like everything else you prize, it must be well cared for.

Your sex glands *(the testicles)* help keep you healthy. They give off something into your blood that makes the voice deep, causes the beard to grow, and gives strength. They also make the sperms — the life cells that pass to the women during sex relations.

Sex relations should be kept for marriage. Between people who aren't married they often lead to shame, sorrow and disease. The public knows this so well that laws forbid sex relations between persons not married to each other. Good morals limit these sex relations to marriage.

Is It All Right for You to Give in to Your Desires?—You wouldn't like to think that the girl you marry had been used by other men. Or that your sweetheart or sister was letting herself be used by someone. You feel a duty to protect her honor. If you want the girl you love and respect to keep her body pure and free from disease, you owe it to her to keep yours the same way.

Nothing is more unfair than to expect her to control her normal desires while you give in to yours. Americans pride themselves on fair play. A good soldier plays fair. Will you?

140

Do You Need Sex Relations?—Some people who don't
know any better may tell you that man needs sex relations to
keep his testicles healthy. This is *not* true. Our best athletes and
fighters avoid sex relations while in training.

Their trainers insist that they do this to save strength and
vigor. The sex organs are not muscles, so exercise can't make
them larger or stronger. In fact, it may even weaken you to use
them too much.

And there's always the danger of getting VENEREAL
DISEASES (V.D.).

You Can't Tell Who is Infected.—Some men think they
can tell if a girl has V.D. just by her looks. Nobody can do this,
not even the doctor. But you can be pretty sure that a prostitute, a pick-up, or a girl who hangs around barrooms has V.D.

Any strange girl who lets a man use her has let other men use
her also. If she has done this very often, she's a natural to have
caught a disease.

How to Avoid Venereal Disease.—The Army can protect
you from many diseases, but you'll have to protect yourself from
syphilis and gonorrhea. The only sure way is to stay away from
women.

If you wait until you marry, you're safe and keep your self-
respect. You also play fair with "the girl back home" whom you
expect to play fair with you.

There's no substitute for morals.

> [War Department, Washington, D.C., *"Sex Hygiene And
> Venereal Disease"* 1942. Prepared under the direction of
> the Surgeon General of the Army. A copy will be furnished
> to each recruit upon enlistment.]

THE SECRETARY OF THE NAVY CHANGES
HIS MIND ABOUT SEX

At an early meeting of those interested in the
control of venereal disease in the army it was suggested that

the most effective way to meet the problem would be for the government to supply public women to the soldiers under a painstaking system of examination and control, as had been done during the recent war with Mexico when the U.S. Government built stockades for the housing of prostitutes and actually shipped women in.

Mr. Abraham Flexner who was present at the meeting declared: "There is no use discussing the merits of regulation. The public will not tolerate the open recognition of prostitution."

In the end his opinion prevailed, and medical men transferred their aspirations to prophylaxis, hoping this means to minimize the danger of venereal contacts.

From the outset the station method of prophylaxis was preferred to the packet and General Orders were promptly issued by the War and Navy Departments requiring all soldiers and sailors who had indulged in illicit intercourse to report promptly to a prophylactic station for early treatment.

Even Secretary of the Navy Daniels, who before the war had been opposed to the issuance of prophylactic packets, capitulated to the plan for early treatment.

In 1915 Secretary of the Navy Daniels wrote to all commanding officers as follows:

"The spectacle of an officer or hospital steward calling up boys in their teens as they are going on leave and handing them these 'preventive packets' is abhorrent to me.

"It is equivalent to the government advising these boys that it is right for them to indulge in an evil which perverts their morals. I would not permit a youth in whom I was interested to enlist in a service that would thus give virtual approval to disobeying the teachings of his parents and the dictates of the highest moral code. You may say that the ideal is raised too high, and we need not expect young men to live up to the ideal of continence. If so, I cannot agree. It is a duty we cannot shirk to point to the true ideal—to chastity, the single standard of morals for men and women."

This was before America's entrance into the great war, before the compelling power of necessity had forced upon military and medical men alike a true realization of the practical cost to the nation of venereal disease.

On May 5, 1918, carried by the tide of public opinion toward prophylaxis, he reversed his position and wrote:

142

"Every man in the Navy is given opportunity to present himself to a medical officer for early treatment and such measures of preventive medicine as may still be possible if he has willfully indulged in a sin against the admonitions of his medical advisers and in spite of the splendid endeavors of the representatives of the Commission on Training Camp Activities."

[Hooker, *Laws of Sex*, pp. 260-61.]

THE PROBLEM WITH SEXUAL PERVERTS
IS THAT THEY ENJOY THE
STATUS QUO

Cases of sexual perversion are very much more frequent than is supposed; but they are very rarely studied by scientific men, and only in exceptional cases do they consult scientific men.

This class of people do not wish to get well.

They are content with their lot, like the majority of opium-eaters and inebriates, and have no occasion to go to a physician; they enjoy their abnormal life, or, if they do not enjoy it, are at least not sufficiently annoyed by it, or are too ashamed of it to attempt any treatment.

There are, as I have recently learned on inquiry, great numbers of such cases in the city of New York.

[George M. Beard, A.M., M.D. (formerly lecturer on nervous diseases in the City University of New York), *Sexual Neurasthenia* (Nervous Exhaustion) — Its Hygiene, Causes, Symptoms, and Treatment (New York: E. B. Treat, 1898). pp. 101-2.]

FEW REALIZE IT, BUT THERE IS MORE VICE, IMMORALITY, AND HARLOTRY GOING AROUND THESE DAYS THAN EVER BEFORE

It is hardly necessary to say that improper sexual conduct is rife among us, and that it is polluting the sanctity of our homes to a degree only superficially appreciated.

The pure, healthy glow of Sexuality, which is the greatest boon to the individual and to the race, becomes a curse when debased by Sensuality.

These two words have become confused in the language of men of the world; so much so, that what we grant to be pre-eminently necessary for the assurance of a virile race — namely, sexual power — has been prostituted by sensuality.

Voluptuousness, of course, has as its indispensable condition the degradation of a large number of women, and it has come to be a turbulent force which is actively consuming a large proportion of the community of every district, annihilating reputations with disgrace, consuming bodies with disease, polluting the sacredness and defiling the sacredness of marriage.

There are few of either sex in this age who do not know that vice and immorality and harlotry exist to a shocking degree; and reticence upon these matters cannot improve our ethics, for sin simply luxuriates in secrecy and ignorance.

[Scott, *Sexual Instinct*, pp. 20-21.]

THERE IS A NAME FOR A MAN WHO IS A SCREAMING VORTEX OF LICENTIOUS LEWDNESS

In the pronounced cases of satyriasis, the individual is the personification of sexuality. In his proximity, everything turns to sex.

144

Every glance, motion or word of his has a sex coloring. He is nothing but a demoniac sex-creature.

Every word he utters has an obscene emotional tone. His exclamations of surprise, fear, anger, etc., all borrowed from the realm of sex.

He is a screaming vortex of licentious lewdness.

A continual lustful scent exudes from him. He is perennially in quest of sexual gratification.

He tries to excite every woman whom he comes in contact with and is himself excited by her.

Moral Consideration is an unknown quantity for him. The inhibitions, normally emanating from the cerebral centre are destroyed in him.

He is continually bent on new sensations.

This picture of the evil spirit of satyriasis is still surpassed by nymphomania.

Never is there uncovered in insane men such an abundance and monstrosity of sexual imagery as in insane women. In dreams and in the dusky twilight of insanity, men and women abandon themselves to their true impulses and desires without the restraining influences of conventionality.

The normal woman has learned by education to hide her true sexual feelings and was forced by tradition to produce in a quite extraordinary way the impression that she herself was nearly nonsexual, and her sexuality is only a concession to the man.

But judging from her sexual emotions and abnormal states the intensity of woman's sexuality is of a higher degree than the man's and herein lies woman's superior morality.

[Talmey, *Love.*]

MEN WITH A LARGE LIBIDO ARE DANGEROUS, AND CERTAIN WOMEN SHOULDN'T BE LET OUT OF THE HOUSE

Libido is the desire for the opposite sex.

A proper amount of libido is normal and desirable. A lack of libido is abnormal. And an excess of libido is also abnormal.

But a good many men are possessed of an excess of libido; it is either congenital or acquired. Some men torture their wives "to death," not literally, but figuratively. Harboring the prevailing idea that a wife has no rights in this respect, that her body is not her own, that she must always hold herself ready to satisfy his abnormal desires, such a husband exercises his marital rights without consideration for the physical condition or the mental feelings of his partner.

Some husbands demand that their wives satisfy them *daily* from one to five or more times a day.

Some wives who happen to be possessed of an equally strong libido do not mind these excessive demands (though in time they are almost sure to feel the evil effects), but if the wife possesses only a moderate amount of sexuality and if she is too weak in body and in will-power to resist her lord and master's demands, her health is often ruined and she becomes a wreck. (Complete abstinence and excessive indulgence often have the same evil end results.)

Some men "kill" four or five women before the fury of their libido is at last moderated.

Of course, it is hard to find out a man's libido beforehand. But if a delicate girl or a woman of moderate sexuality has reasons to suspect that a man is possessed of an abnormally excessive libido, she would do well to think twice before taking the often irretrievable step.

Excessive Libido in Women — Just as we have impotent and excessively libidinous men, so we have frigid and excessively libidinous women.

A wife possessed of an excessive libido is a terrible calamity for a husband of a normal or moderate sexuality.

Many a libidinous wife has driven her husband, especially if she is young and he is old, to a premature grave.

And "grave" is used in the literal, not figurative, sense of the word.

It would be a good thing if a man could find out the character of his future wife's libido before marriage. Unfortunately, it is impossible. At best, it can only be guessed at. But a really excessive libido on the part of either husband or wife should constitute a valid ground for divorce.

WHEN NATURE'S LAWS *are* VIOLATED

When the libido in woman is so excessive that she *cannot* control her passion, and forgetting religion, morality, modesty, custom and possible social consequences, she offers herself to every man she meets, we use the term nymphomania.

Nymphomaniac women should not be permitted to marry or run around loose, but should be confined to institutions in which they can be subjected to proper treatment.

[Robinson, *Woman*, pp. 235-38.]

HOW TO TELL WHEN A NYMPHOMANIAC IS TRYING TO GET YOUR ATTENTION

The intensity of her desire being greater, her higher chastity is more laudable. And in certain periods, such as pregnancy and lactation, when woman is really more or less non sexual, her chastity has no merit.

But in the other states of her life when woman's desires possess a higher degree of intensity, her chastity is of a superior kind.

Sexual inclination is normally increased immediately before and after the menses. Still, it may be laid down as a rule that an overweening sexual desire in a woman, considering her natural modesty and coyness, should arouse suspicion of its pathological significance.

The nymphomaniac woman seeks to attract men by indecent language, by lascivious conduct, by personal adornment, perfumes, talk of marriage, by the exhibition of feet, legs, neck, breasts and other parts of her body, and, at the height of her excitement, invitation to intercourse.

She is often seen in a physician's office and desires gynecological examinations for the gratification of her excitement.

The best and most careful rearing of girls suffering from nymphomania, cannot save them from downfall. In their wild passion, casting all moral and social considerations aside they

148

throw themselves into the arms of sin. The more they abandon themselves to the gratification of their lust, the greater is the desire of their morbidly excited nerve-centers for lecherous satisfaction. The woman loses control of her passions and cannot restrain herself from onanism or copulation. She becomes obsessed in sexual gratification.

[Talmey, *Love*.]

INTELLIGENT MEN SAVE THEIR PRECIOUS BODILY FLUIDS; OR, SPERM CAN HELP YOUR HEAD

A man will seldom wish to perpetuate himself in more than from one to six children; hence a larger use for his powers of virility lies in revivifying and strengthening his force in other directions.

One writer expresses the subject in the following wholesome language:

> *A man who conserves all his forces and allows no prodigal waste of seminal secretions during the age of virility receives a sure reward. His frame becomes more closely knit, his step more sturdy and elastic, his voice rich, harmonious and magnetic, his mind clearer, his judgment more reliable. He can endure a greater strain of business or study as he goes on in years, and in every way is the reliable man.*
> *This may in large measure be attributed to the absorption and assimilation of the conserved sperm. A large quantity may be taken up by the brain and expended in throught.*
> *No uneasiness need be felt if, after strenuous mental exertion, there should be a temporary arrest of the secretion. Excessive manual labor also, under some circumstances, arrests the secretion, and both body and brain may be affected thereby.*

149

The depressing effect upon the system of tobacco, alcohol, opium and chloral prevents the secretion and assimilation of sperm, robbing both mind and body.

It may be that the widespread tobacco and alcohol habits among men are the chief sources of sexual abnormalities. These have their origin in minds undisciplined to self-control.

[Greer, *Wholesome Woman.*]

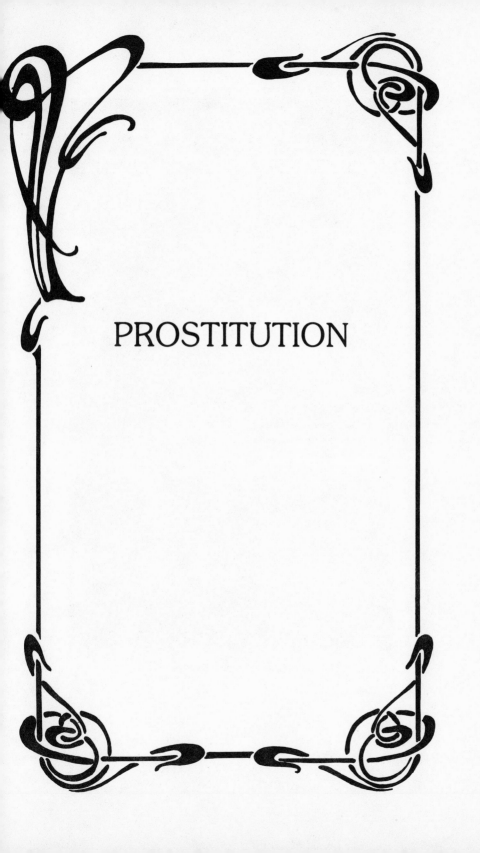

PROSTITUTION

HOMELESS AND FRIENDLESS.

152

PROSTITUTES HAVE DEEP VOICES AND CRIMINAL TRAITS. BUT LIVE TO A GOOD AGE AND ENJOY VIGOROUS HEALTH

Lombroso, Dr. Pauline Tarnowsky, and other physiologists who have investigated the physiology of the prostitute, state that the class exhibit some of the physical and mental peculiarities of criminals.

Lombroso finds that criminals and prostitutes are lacking in sensibility to pain, as well as in general sensibility. There are often masculine traits in prostitutes, but perhaps the most noticeable of these qualities have been acquired through the nature of an occupation which involves assertiveness and self-protection.

It has been noticed that many prostitutes speak with a deep voice, a fact attributed to the effect of sexual excess upon the larynx.

It is in the nervous system of the class that we must look for marked abnormalities. The prostitute is often mentally feeble, morbidly emotional and prone to outbursts of rage. She is readily moved to shed tears.

She weeps with apparent contrition at an evangelical tea meeting, or she is affected by the solumn ritual, the splendid pomp, and the singing of the choir in the cathedral. But only in rare instances is she deeply impressed and morally influenced by religion.

The charitable persons who engage in rescue work are seldom

153

successful in subduing the levity and frivolity of the women who enter the homes. They are difficult to convert.

A young man who endeavored earnestly to reform the prostitutes of the Borough district of London was repeatedly taunted by them for his chastity, and on one occasion a number of girls assaulted him indecently.

Prostitutes regard men as their prey, as enemies who must be outwitted and plundered. Comparatively few of the women have scruples against robbing the men who accompany them. The few charges of thefts in brothels which are brought into court are only a small portion of the cases.

Many of these women lure old, feeble men, and victims in a drunken state to low neighborhoods, where they are robbed by male associates, the cullies and bullies who swarm in great cities.

Probably half of the number of prostitutes have sham "husbands," men of the vilest dregs of humanity, who, in return for their so-called "protection," demand a share of every fee received by the woman. The affection which the prostitute often evinces toward the ruffian with whom she lives is a pathetic instance of the womanly desire for the love and sympathetic companionship of man.

She attaches herself to a drunken wastrel whose fist is often raised to fell her.

Physicians concur that the general health of prostitutes is much better than that of female factory workers and all women who lead sedentary lives. Dr. Acton says: "I shall be borne out by the concurrent testimony of all observers in the statement that no class of females is so free from general diseases as the prostitutes."

Notwithstanding the risks of syphilis, many of the women live to a good age and may be said to enjoy vigorous health.

Three years is said to be the average time during which women engage in mercenary promiscuous intercourse. At the end of that period, many marry, and others obtain occupation as waitresses, barmaids, and minor actresses.

Even the most dissipated and thoughtless men speak of prostitution as an evil, though they consider that the evil is a necessary one.

The opinion is growing that hetairism can be greatly lessened by increasing the facilities for obtaining the only natural and healthy gratification of sexual passion in unions of affection. But marriage under the present state of the laws and public opinion does not, and cannot, afford an adequate remedy for prostitution.

To prove this it is only needful to recognize the fact that married men are the principal consorts of prostitutes.

[Mortimer, *Human Love*, pp. 164-69.]

IT IS NOT WIDELY RECOGNIZED THAT HARLOTS ARE PROMISCUOUS AND SHAMELESS. YET IT SHOULD BE NOTED THAT THEY HAVE HEARTS OF GOLD

Men of high intelligence may frequently be heard to say that they feel safe going to the better grade of bawdy houses, since it is the business of the inmates to keep themselves clean.

Undoubtedly one is less liable to contract disease from a professional strumpet than from an immoral servant-girl, shop-girl, or actress, because the latter are strumpets in secret, and practice no precautions; but the choice is only relative, for all loose women are necessarily most unclean.

By sinking to a depth of infamy far below the level of any examples to be found among the brutes, the unchaste members of the human family have transmitted the filthy venereal diseases through the ages, while the lower animals are exempt.

Even among the most degraded human beings there is an instinctive feeling of self-consciousness while in the sexual embrace, while the brutes are entirely free from all modesty, and, if not frightened, will not hesitate to copulate before witnesses.

This feeling of shame partly explains why venereal affections are called "secret diseases."

There is no animal, not even the swine, which from a bacteriological point of view can for a moment be compared in filth and repulsiveness to a prostitute.

155

When one considers what she is, no prostitute is attractive; and a visual, digital and microscopical examination of her sexual apparatus and its secretions would cool the ardor of a satyr, if he were capable of appreciating the scientific procedures.

A gentleman recently related in the presence of the writer that several years since he was with a very attractive young prostitute, who boasted to him of having received $110 on that single day.

Overcome with disgust at such a striking proof that harlots must be promiscuous, he has never visited one since.

"The supposition that a prostitute submits to but one act of prostitution every day is ridiculously small. No woman could pay her board, dress, and live in the expensive manner common among the class, upon the money she would receive from one visitor daily; even two visitors is a very low estimate, and four is very far from an unreasonably large one."[1]

By frequent douches, astringent washes, and perfumes, the careful harlot may deceive her paramour into the belief that she is all that his fancy and passion could desire; but chronic and filthy discharges flow freely from the whole tribe, and the arts of the *toilette* only conceal the external evidence of their disorders.

A very good damper to the longing of one who desires to go into a brothel would be to stand outside for a time and observe the kind of men whom he is to follow — silly fops, diseased and rotten men, worn-out old men, married men, unmarriageable men.

While we have been so positive in proclaiming that loose women are diseased and loathsome, yet we do not wish to be understood as being too severe on these poor creatures.

It is a hard thing at best for any woman, more especially if equipped for it, to be compelled to earn her own living in competition with men who are often brutal to her; for circumstances and disposition make it harder for some than others.

These prostitutes are not soulless creatures, and their hearts are by no means barren of good.

Many of them, indeed, have kind and honest natures, are self-sacrificing in their devotion to each other when trouble or sickness comes, and often have as good sentiments as many other more fortunate girls.

[1] Sanger, "History of Prostitution," P.599.

[Scott, *Sexual Instinct*, pp. 83-85.]

PROSTITUTION PLAYS AN IMPORTANT
ROLE IN REDUCING THE NATION'S
UNEMPLOYMENT

It is erroneous to assume that prostitution is a vice peculiar to civilization, or that it is restricted entirely to women. Prostitution is found in every stage of human existence from the lowest to the highest.

Woodruff estimates about one million prostitutes in this country. Roe asserts that the average life of these girls is about five years. This means that two hundred thousand prostitutes die every year in the United States and are replaced by new ones.

[Talmey, *Love.*]

UNLIKE RESTRICTED SOCIAL ORGANIZATIONS,
BROTHELS WELCOME ALL NEW
MEMBERS

The Brothel— Who Are the Guests?

The gambler, the thief, the policy dealer, the ruffian; and with these the college student, the bank clerk, the member of the fashionable club; aye, and also the father of the family,the husband of the pure wife, the head of the firm, the member of the church; all these, every night in our great cities.

Can any of these think to escape the contamination? Vain chimera. It is as certain as death.

If nothing else remains, the moral stain is indelible.

[Shannon, *Personal Help*, p. 227.]

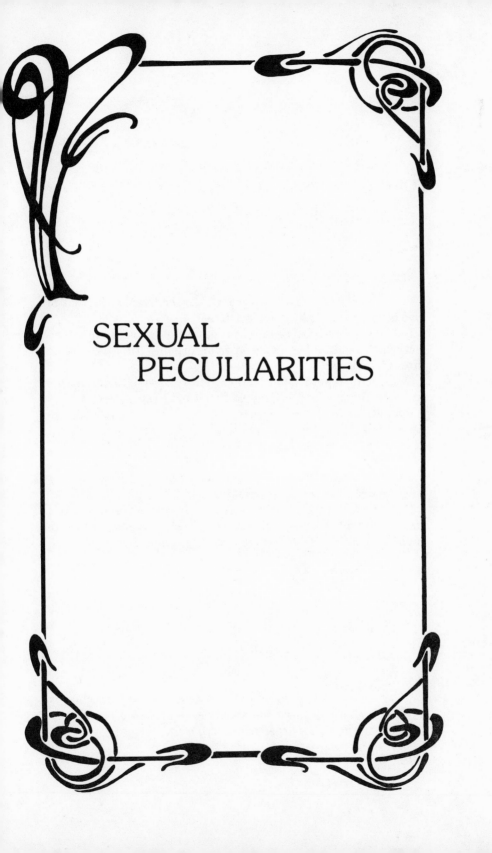

SEXUAL
PECULIARITIES

FORGET THE WAY YOU FEEL IN YOUR HEART— DO YOU LOVE HER WITH ALL YOUR LIVER?

The ancient theory that the liver is the seat of love is not without physiological data.

Solomon alludes in the seventh chapter of Proverbs to the effect which amative excess has upon his organ—"till a dart strike through his liver."

In the thirteenth Ode, Horace declares to Lydia that his "inflamed liver swells with bile difficult to be repressed."

An indifference to the passion of love, and even a total inability to understand the force of the impulse in others, may result in some cases from disease of the liver.

The man or woman who becomes suddenly insensible to the attraction of the opposite sex, may have been erotic during youth and the earlier years of maturity.

A serious liver complaint will modify and change a man's views upon many things, and there is therefore good reason to suppose that such disorders may destroy sex-feeling.

[Mortimer, *Human Loves*, pp. 189-90.]

LOVE IS A STRANGE FEELING IN YOUR SOLAR PLEXUS

There are in the cavity of the body bunches of knots of nerves, through the spontaneous action of which the functions of the bodily organs are carried on.

160

The greatest of these, and the one upon which the others all unite, lies back of the navel, and is called in scientific language, the *solar plexus*.

This is the great emotional center of man, and is the real organ which is meant by the term "heart" as the seat of love.

In the Bible phrase, "His heart melteth in the midst of his bowels," this location which I have pointed out is clearly indicated. In general, also, the whole region from the navel to the breasts is signified by this term. As the physical heart is powerfully affected by this great nerve center, and as the ancients did not have skill enough in anatomy to distinguish the solar plexus, it is easy to see how the name of the physical organ came to be applied to this emotional center, which is really something quite other.

The solar plexus is the throne of love. There this deep and tender emotion centers, and from thence it radiates.

But also temperament centers there. Temperament is the quality of the vitality, as mind is its form.

Love is not in the brain.

Love is not in the loins.

Love is in the temperament as centering upon the solar plexus.

[Shannon, *Nature's Secrets*, p. 89.]

IF YOU PUT ONE AMBITIOUS MAN IN A ROOM WITH ALL THE SINGLE WOMEN IN THE WORLD, YOU COULD BE IN FOR A BIG SURPRISE

It is estimated that there are somewhere between two and five hundred million sperms in a single average ejaculation. Each single one of these (in healthy men) is capable of fertilizing a woman's egg-cell and giving rise to a new human being.

(Thus by a single ejaculation one man might fertilize nearly all the marriageable women in the world!)

[Stopes, *Married Love*, p. 59.]

YOU CAN GET MORE OUT OF SEX IF YOU
USE YOUR NOSE

Women, says Hagen, are like the flowers who spread their intoxicating fragrance during dawn and dusk — as the first rays of the rising and the last rays of the setting sun.

With some the sweetest odors emanate during night-time.

Before a thunderstorm, when the air is close, the feminine odor is particularly pronounced. The transpiration of lean women is less pronounced than in the stout, who possess usually large sudoriparous pores and sebaceous glands.

Brunettes have a stronger feminine odor than blondes, and both are *surpassed by the red-haired.*

Before and after conjugation, the natural body odor of the woman is more intense. Two of the author's patients were reported to exhale an odor somewhat resembling that of onions, immediately after the orgasm.

[Talmey, *Love.*]

ONE SURE-FIRE WAY TO MAKE A RUSSIAN
WOMAN REALLY HAPPY

The Persians and Russians regard beating as a peculiar *sign of love.*

Russian women are never more pleased than when receiving a drubbing at the hands of their husbands.

[Parke, *Sexuality.*]

PROMISE HER ANYTHING, BUT GIVE
HER SWEAT

Professor Most relates the case of a young peasant who had excited many a chaste girl, sexually, and easily gained his end, by carrying a handkerchief under his arm while dancing, and afterwards wiping his partner's perspiring face with it.

[Parke, *Sexuality.*]

162

SEX CAN HAVE UNEXPECTED
THERAPEUTIC BENEFITS

Following is an extract from a history in my possession: Mr. and Mrs._____had been happily married fifty-five years, were still lovers. Mrs._____ascribed their many years of perfect happiness together to complete sex adjustment.

They had intercourse two or three times a week, which she always enjoyed as much as her husband.

She had a shock at the age of seventy-eight and was ill several weeks. One morning, though conscious, she was very weak, and had a subnormal temperature.

The Dr. said she could not live twenty-four hours. She selected the dress she wished to be buried in. The husband was heartbroken.

The following morning her temperature was normal and she was improved in every way.

It was then learned that she and her husband had had intercourse during the night.

She continued to gain, and died two years later at the age of eighty, outliving her husband, who died one year after the event recorded, at the age of seventy-six.

[W.F. Robie, M.D., *The Art of Love* (1921).]

A DOCTOR OFFERS AN INGENIOUS CURE
FOR NYMPHOMANIA

[Nymphomania] is an abnormal, intense and overmastering desire in women for the sexual act. It is often so great as to cause the woman to solicit on the street, not as the streetwalker does for the money that is in it, but for the purpose of gratification only.

Such victims are unfit for matrimony.

Yet, if the case has not gone too far, matrimony might be a sovereign cure.

[Dr. T. J. Pierce, *Sex Manual: A Scientific, Physiological, and Hygienic Study of the Sex Question* (1922).]

A MAN WITH LARGE EQUIPMENT MAY FIND
SOME DOORS CLOSED TO HIM

Prostitutes, as a rule, have a horror and dread of the man with a big and long penis, and prefer by far the less ostentatiously decorated individual, whose member reaches the clitoris equally well, producing the same pleasure without the attending pain, and, best of all, for their purposes at least, producing the same revenue.

This statement, I know, takes a spoke out of the wheel of the fellow who prides himself on the weight and caliber of his artillery, and puts a premium rather upon small and active "quick firers."

[Parke, *Sexuality.*]

YOU, TOO, CAN BE BETTER ENDOWED

The abnormal sexual appetite common to the adult man is due to a number of causes, among which may be named stimulating food and drink, and a continuous dwelling upon sexual subjects.

> *If a man engages in physical exercise, the muscles become developed; if he engages in intellectual study, the brain becomes enlarged and developed, and if his sexual organs are constantly in a state of excitement from allowing his attention to be continually directed to this sphere, then he must become abnormally developed,*

says Dr. Elliott.

[Greer, *Wholesome Woman.*]

164

HOW TO TAKE THE MEASURE OF A MAN:
A MATTER OF INCHES

The penis is located at the lowest part of the abdomen, just above the junction of the thighs.

Its normal length when erect is about one-twelth of the height of the body, that is, there should be one inch of length for every foot of height so that a man who is five feet six inches tall would normally have a male organ 5 1/2 inches in length when in the erect state.

[Charles A. Clinton, M.D., *Sex Behavior in Marriage* (1935).]

DOES SHE OR DOESN'T SHE? EVEN HER
HAIRDRESSER MAY NOT KNOW
FOR SURE

The part of the body upon which the sex organs, male and female, are located is known as the pubic region.

It is covered with hair, which, in both sexes, extends well up the lower belly.

This is known as pubic hair, and in general, corresponds in quality and quantity to the hair upon the individual head, being coarse or fine, soft or bristly, to match the head covering in each case.

This hair is usually more or less curly, and forms a covering an inch or more in depth over the whole pubic region. In occasional cases, this hair is straight and silky, and sometimes grows to great length, instances known, in some women, where it has extended to the knees.

A well-grown and abundant supply of fine pubic hair is a possession highly prized by women, of which they are justly proud, though few of them would acknowledge the fact, even to themselves.

None the less, it is a fact.

[Long, *Sane Sex.*]

165

SAILORS' WIVES USE AN EFFECTIVE FORMULA TO KEEP YOUNG. IT COULD WORK JUST AS WELL FOR OTHER WOMEN

The sea captains whose homes dot our Atlantic Coast not only manage with great courage and skill one of the most important interests of civilized life, but by their long absence and brief home visits, they involuntarily contribute something infinitely better than their professional industry — even a better breed of human beings.

Everybody has been struck with the number of successful men and women who trace their origin to these captain's settlements, but very few have attributed this superiority to its true source. And certainly no one can go to Martha's Vineyard, or any similar community of sailors' wives, without being struck with the singular and exceptional freshness of the women.

They have not been drained to the dregs by conjugal debauchery.

[Lewis, *Chastity.*]

GONORRHEA FOR FUN AND PROFIT

In some women, this disease causes little inconvenience but in others it is very serious, putting the woman under the care of a physician for several weeks.

It is exceedingly contagious. One woman is sufficient to infect 100 men.

I know a doctor in a lumber camp who had very little business although the camp employed 200 men. He went to a large city and finding a very beautiful woman who was infected with this disease, offered her a bribe to take up residence in the lumber town.

In a few days, he had all he could do.

It was a clever move, but far from being an honorable one.

[Pierce, *Sex Manual.*]

166

A FRIGID WOMAN IS ALSO A VIRTUOUS WOMAN

Some women experience an entire absence of the desire for the sexual act. There are many contributing causes for this trouble. The main one I have discovered is self-abuse.

This is very hard to discuss and very hard to cure. If the trouble can be discovered and cured in time, the girl may be saved, but if not, her life is sure to be a wreck.

Such girls are invariably virtuous. They could not be seduced into having normal intercourse.

[Pierce, *Sex Manual.*]

THE GROCER'S SHELF IS TEEMING WITH POTENT APHRODISIACS

Everything which inflames one appetite is likely to arouse the other also.

Pepper, mustard, ketchup and Worcestershire sauce — shun them all.

And even salt, in any but the smallest quantity, is objectionable; it is such a goad toward carnalism that the ancient fable depicted Venus as born of the salt sea-wave.

[Lewis, *Chastity.*]

BEWARE OF EXCITING YOUR NEIGHBORHOOD CLERGYMEN

Our most profound disgust is justly excited when we hear of laxity of morals in clergyman.

We naturally feel that one whose calling is to teach his fellow-

167

men the way of truth and right and purity, should himself be free from taint of immorality.

But when we consider how these ministers are fed, we cannot suppress a momentary disposition to excuse, in some degree, their fault. When the minister goes out to tea, he is served with the richest cake, the choicest jellies, the most pungent sauces, and the finest of fine-flour bread-stuffs.

Little does the indulgent hostess dream that she is ministering to the inflammation of passions which may imperil the virtue of her daughter, or even her own *(sic)*.

Salacity once aroused, even in a minister, allows no room for reason or for conscience. If women wish to preserve the virtue of their ministers, let them feed them more in accordance with the laws of health.

Ministers are not immaculate.

[Kellog, *Plain Facts.*]

THE SINGLE GREATEST THREAT TO OUR CRIMINAL-JUSTICE SYSTEM IS A JURY OF FETISHISTS.

The sexual impulse is not the same in all persons. Those of sanguine temperaments are voluptuous, romantic and given to fetishism.

By fetishism is meant that peculiar tendency of a lover to worship or love his mistress's hair, foot, stocking, or some other part of her body or clothing.

That exaggerated state of the normal sexual feeling which made the knight of the Middle Ages drink Tokay from his lady's slipper, carry her colors on his lance, or a lock of her hair in his bosom; and which, making a fetish of female beauty, stands today as the most threatening factor in our modern system of jury-trial as it relates to female criminals.

It is hard to make such a man convict a female criminal, if she be attractive, for any crime, however flagrant.

[Parke, *Sexuality.*]

168

CIRCUMCISION: THE UNKINDEST
CUT OF ALL

Circumcision is the cutting off of the foreskin. It has been handed down to us from early Bible times.

It is a Jewish ceremony. . . .

The Jews circumcise all male children six days after birth. It is then a very simple operation but if delayed too late in life it is not so simple.

[Pierce, *Sex Manual.*]

IT JUST ISN'T THE SAME WHEN YOU
WEAR GOLDBEATER'S SKIN ON
YOUR PENIS

Probably the method of prevention which has come into the widest use is the employment of the "cundum" *(sic)* or sheath, for the penis during the sexual act.

This article is made usually of goldbeater's skin, or rubber, exceedingly thin, while fairly efficacious in preventing impregnation, as well as infection, is yet, as a witty lady once remarked, "A cobweb against danger and a cuirass against pleasure."

And beside the pleasure derivable from such an intercourse, it lacks every element of the physical joy and fruition the naked congress possesses; and, to use a homely illustration, is a good bit like going in swimming with your clothes on.

[Parke, *Sexuality.*]

HOW TO TELL IF A "NICE" GIRL IS THE
VIRGIN SHE CLAIMS TO BE

The slipping off recalls to my mind a story told me by a patient, a young man, who, after prolonged solicitation,

at last got a "nice young lady" to consent to the act on condition, only that he would use "one of those rubber bags she had
heard of."

Of course, he joyfully consented, and in the course of the
connection, the instrument slipping off, he reached his finger in
to recover it, and succeeded, to his infinite disgust, in fishing out
no fewer than *six others.*

[Parke, *Sexuality.*]

LOLITA MUST HAVE
BEEN A BRUNETTE

It has been observed that in girls the occurrence of puberty is earlier in brunettes than in blondes.

[Kellog, *Plain Facts.*]

SOME FACTS ABOUT THE SEX LIVES OF
JEWISH MEN

A good deal has been said concerning the hot
blood of warm climates, and on the whole it appears true that
people who inhabit these climates have a more violent and more
precocious sexual temperament than those who live in cold
regions.

But this is not a racial character.

The Jews, who have preserved their race unaltered in all
climates and under all possible conditions of existence, furnish
an object lesson which is particularly appropriate to decide the
question.

The traits of their character are reflected in their sexual life.
Their sexual appetites are generally strong and their love is
distinguished by great family attachment. Their sexual life is

170

BRUNETTE—A TYPE OF BEAUTY

also influenced by their mercantile spirit, and we find them everywhere connected with the traffic of women and prostitution.

They are not very jealous and are much addicted to concubinage, at the same time remaining affectionate to their wife and family.

[Forel, *Sexual Question*, p. 189.]

IF YOU REALLY NEED A LOVER AND CAN'T FIND ONE, TRY THIS APPEALING ALTERNATIVE

Artificial Erotism. The Artificial Penis and Cunnus — As to the artificial penis, it is almost as old as the natural one.

In China, it is made chiefly of colophene, mixed with certain vegetable oils to render it permanently supple and flexible; and, sometimes beautifully colored, is both widely used and publicly sold.

The use of the artifical penis, as well as the *cunnus succedaneus* or corresponding female organ, for the use of men, can be traced back in medical writings to the most primitive ages of Egyptian, Babylonian and Persian luxury.

The Latin *phallus*, or *fascinum*, and the Indian *lingam*, are known in France as the *godemiche*, and in Italy as the *diletto*, the original of the modern *dildo*, under which latter name it is usually sold in America.

The *cunnus succedaneus*, from *cuneus* — a wedge — and *succedaneus* — artificial, or substitutory — from the former of which we also get the vulgar epithet applied to the female genitals — is known in England as a *merkin*, meaning originally, according to Bailey's Dictionary, "counterfeit hair for a woman's private parts."

The term *cunnus* has evident reference to the wedge-like shape of the vulvar orifice; and to those who are not fastidious in such matters, or too poor to keep the genuine article, especially

172

in the style which modern fashion demands, the *cunnus suc-cedaneus* has much to recommend it.

It is never associated with objectionable garrulity, never diseased, always open for engagements, and needs only a few mothballs occasionally instead of an expensive wardrobe, to keep it in thorough condition and repair.

The artificial penis possesses similarly good properties. It is always true to the lady who courts it; doesn't get intoxicated and balky; needs no coaxing; and its size and length may be regulated to suit her taste, a matter not always possible with the normal article.

[Parke, *Sexuality*, p. 383.]

STOP ME IF YOU'VE HEARD THIS
MEDICAL ANECDOTE

In China there are special houses of male pro-stitution; as also in Paris, London and New York; and in most of the American and French cities both men and women are kept for whichever form of intercourse is preferred by the patron.

I cannot resist an anecdote in connection with this custom.

A wealthy young man in New York, who kept a regular harem of boys for this purpose, was in the habit of treating them liberally to champagne before selecting one for his nocturnal pleasure.

And a new boy having been introduced, filled with champagne, and in this condition subjected to the usual process, when asked next morning by one of the other boys how he liked getting drunk on champagne replied, rubbing his posterior playfully—"I like it all right, but doesn't it make your behind sore?"

[Parke, *Sexuality*, p. 251.]

EXHIBITIONISM; OR, CARRYING SHOW AND TELL A BIT TOO FAR

There is a class of individuals, especially men, whose sole sexual desire consists in masturbating in the presence of women.

They lie in wait behind some wall or bush, and masturbate openly when women pass that way. In these subjects an orgasm is only produced when they are observed by women. As soon as ejaculation has occurred they fly to avoid the police. They never attempt to molest the women whose presence excites them to this performance.

These cases are not uncommon and naturally cause much scandal, so that poor wretches seldom escape the police. These unfortunate persons who sometimes hold high social positions, have often been previously convicted, but cannot as a rule overcome their passion, which has much worse consequences for them than for the women and children whom they frighten and annoy.

Exhibitionism is not rare among insane women and I have myself treated two typical cases. I do not know whether it occurs in women of sound mind, but at all events they cannot be addicted to it without running great risk.

[Forel, *Sexual Questions*, p. 241.]

A SMART WOMAN IS JUST AS CAREFUL IN HER DENTIST'S CHAIR AS IN THE LADIES' ROOM

But besides the venereal sources of infection the woman must guard against the non-venereal sources.

Do not ever, if you can avoid it, use a public toilet. If you are forced to use it, protect yourself by putting some paper over the seat.

Do not use a public drinking cup. If you have to use one, keep

174

SAFETY FIRST

your lips away from the rim. One can learn to drink without touching the rim of the glass or cup with the lips.

Do not under any circumstances use a public towel. The roller towel is a menace to health and should be forbidden in every part of the country.

If you have to sleep in a hotel or in a strange bed, make sure that the linen is clean and fresh. Never sleep on bed linen which has been used by a stranger.

Be sure that your dentist is a careful, up-to-date man, and sterilizes his instruments carefully.

Many a case of syphilis has been transmitted by a dentist's instrument.

[Robinson, *Woman,* pp. 178-79.]

IF A MAN LOVES A WOMAN, HE MUST BE PREPARED TO LOWER HIMSELF FOR HER

As a rule, the orgasm does not come at the same time in both mates. In the woman it is generally induced later than in the man. The woman must therefore be first prepared for conjugation.

The man should not attempt penetration until his wife's passions have become moist with the pre-coital flow. Such dalliance has been described by some ascetics as beneath a man's dignity.

But nothing is low if born of love.

[Talmey, *Love.*]

IT IS WISE NOT TO JUDGE A MAN BY THE SIZE OF HIS PRIZE

Variation In Size [*of penis*]— The dimensions of this organ vary in different persons.

In the flaccid or soft state, the organ varies from four to six or seven inches.

176

No one should take the size of this organ as a safe criterion by which to judge either his virility or his reproductive capacity.

Quack doctors lay great stress upon the small size of this organ as evidence of great injury done by the practice of the secret sin.

Since a large per cent of men have practiced the secret sin, and since the organ varies so much in different men, and since so many men are ignorant of these variations, this offers to the quack doctor a most favorable opportunity to prey upon the hard earnings of young men.

[Shannon, *Personal Help*, pp. 27-28.]

ALL MEN ARE NOT CREATED EQUAL.
THE NUMBER OF STROKES
DIFFERS FOR FOLKS

The fact that there are men who for several years can copulate several times a day proves to what extent sexual power varies in men.

Sexual excitation and desire may sometimes attain such a degree that they are repeated a few minutes after ejaculation. It is not rare for a man to perform coitus ten or fifteen times in a single night, in brothels and elsewhere, although such excess borders on the domain of pathology.

I know a case in which coitus was performed thirty times.

I was once consulted by an old woman of 65 who complained of the insatiable sexual appetite of her husband, aged 73! He awakened her every morning at three o'clock to have connection, before going to work.

Not content with this, he repeated the performance every evening and often also after the mid-day meal.

Inversely, I have seen healthy looking husbands, at the age of greatest sexual power, accuse themselves of excess for having cohabited with their wives once a month or less.

[Forel, *Sexual Question*, pp. 82-83.]

ONE MALE ORGAN IS CAPABLE OF EXTENDING ITSELF MORE THAN ANY OTHER. CAN YOU GUESS WHAT THE LITTLE DEVIL IS CALLED?

The sex organs in a male human being consists, broadly speaking, of the penis and the testicles.

All these are located at the base of the abdomen, between the thighs and on the forward part of the body.

The penis is a fleshy, muscular organ, filled with most sensitive nerves, and blood vessels that are capable of extension to a much greater degree than any of their similars in other parts of the body.

The testicles are two kidney shaped glands, not far from the size of a large hickory nut, and are contained in a sort of sack, or pocket, called the scrotum, which is made for their comfortable and safe carrying.

[Long, *Sane Sex*, pp. 40-42.]

IF A WOMAN APPEARS SKITTISH, IT IS WISE TO ASSURE HER THAT THINGS MAY NOT BE AS LARGE AS THEY APPEAR AT FIRST BLUSH

Some apprehension is occasionally expressed about the size of the genitalia, and in general it may be said of the male organ that it rarely, if indeed ever, occurs that the member is of such monstrous size that it cannot be accommodated.

When it is recalled that a child, which is certainly many times larger than a penis, is passed out of the parts, no fear need be entertained about capaciousness if ordinary care be exercised.

As a matter of fact, the chief effect of the dimensions of the parts is the impression which they make upon the mind of the observer.

[C. W. Malchow, M.D. (formerly professor of proctology and associate in clinical medicine, Hamline University College of Physicians and Surgeons), *The Sexual Life* — Embracing the Natural Sexual Impulse, Normal Sexual Habits, and Propagation, together with Sexual Physiology and Hygiene (St. Louis: Mosby, 1907, 1928), pp. 182-83.]

THE SECRET SIN

HOW TO SPOT YOUR NEIGHBORHOOD ONANIST: TELLTALE SIGNS THAT HE'S BECOME HIS OWN BEST FRIEND

At the first glance the onanist presents an aspect of languor, weakness, and thinness. The countenance is pale, sunken, flabby, often leaden, or more or less livid, with a dark circle around the sunken eyes, which are dull, and lowered or averted.

The voice is feeble and hoarse; there are oppression, panting, and fatigue on the least exertion.

Sometimes the body is bent, and often there are the characteristics of decreptitude joined to the habits and pretensions of youth.

Such is the physical degradation of the masturbator.

Enough has been said to enable any intelligent observer to recognize the confirmed onanist.

Occasional offenders manifest the same characteristics in different degrees, and it would be difficult for even such to escape the practiced eye of the physician.

Perhaps the most constant and invariable, as well as earliest signs, are the downcast, averted glance, and the disposition to solitude.

But while the physical symptoms are so grave, the moral degradation goes even further. Prominent characteristics are: loss of memory and intelligence, morose and unequal disposition, aversion, or indifference to legitimate pleasures and sports, mental abstractions, stupid stolidity, etc.

[A Physician, *Satan.*]

182

A PARTIAL LIST OF THE PHYSICAL RAVAGES OF THE SECRET SIN

Physical Effects:

1. The victim is subject to loss of spirit, weakness of memory, despondency and apathy.

2. Anaemia and facial acne are common.

3. There is loss of manly bearing and proneness to blush.

4. The path leads to imbecility and premature senility.

5. The countenance and demeanor stamp the onanist as an object of reasonable suspicion.

6. His genitals bear the marks of his degrading practice.

7. His digestion and heart action are disturbed, and he becomes a moody, apprehensive, hypochondriacal invalid, if not a gross pervert.

[Scott, *Sexual Instinct*, p. 424.]

GIRLS DO IT TOO—YOU CAN TELL FROM THEIR BLANCHED CHEEKS

The same signs which betray the boy will make known the girl addicted to this vice.

The bloodless lips, the dull, heavy eye surrounded with dark rings, the nerveless hand, the blanched cheek, the short breath, the old, faded look, the weakened memory, and silly irritability tell the story all too plainly. The same evil result follows, ending perhaps in death, or worse, insanity.

[Melendy, *Perfect Womanhood.*]

183

CRIMINAL POLLUTERS DON'T NEED A HELPING HAND; THEY'D RATHER DO IT THEMSELVES

If illicit commerce of the sexes is a heinous sin, self-pollution, or masturbation, is a crime doubly abominable.

As a sin against nature, it has no parallel except in sodomy (see Gen. 19:5; Judges 19:22).

It is the most dangerous of all sexual abuses because it is the most extensively practiced. The vice consists of an excitement of the genital organs produced otherwise than in the natural way.

It is known by the terms: self-pollution, self-abuse, masturbation, onanism, manustupration, voluntary pollution, and solitary or secret vice.

Its frequent repetition fastens it upon the victim with a fascination almost irresistible.

Even though no warning may have been given, the transgressor seems to know, instinctively, that he is committing a great wrong, for he carefully hides his practice from observation.

In solitude he pollutes himself, and with his own hand blights all his prospects for both this world and the next.

Even after being solemnly warned, he will often continue this worse than beastly practice, deliberately forfeiting his right to health and happiness for a moment's mad sensuality.

[Kellog, *Plain Facts.*]

ONE ANSWER TO THE SCOURGE OF SELF-ABUSE MAY BE FEDERAL REGULATION OF HANDS

According to Dr. Franck, "Masturbators are not only a charge upon society, but are even dangerous," and this celebrated physician exhorts governments to exercise over them the most active supervision.

[A Physician, *Satan.*]

184

FOR THE REST OF THE WORLD, THE WORST VICE IS MALE MASTURBATION. IN THE UNITED STATES, IT COMES IN SECOND

Viewing the world over, this shameful and criminal act is the most frequent, as well as the most fatal, of all vices.

In our country, however, it is second in frequency — though not, surely, in importance — only to the crime of libertinism. It is encountered in all ages, from the infant in cradle to the old man groaning upon his pallet.

But it is from the age of fourteen to twenty that its ravages are most frequent and most deplorable.

Nothing but a sense of inexorable duty, in the hope of effecting a radical reform by awakening the alarm of parents and teachers to the enormous frequency and horrible consequences of this revolting crime could induce the author to enter upon the sickening revelation.

[A Physician, *Satan.*]

A DISTINGUISHED GERMAN PHYSICIAN DESCRIBES THE HEART- BREAK OF MASTURBATION. IT ISN'T A PRETTY PICTURE

A distinguished German physician, Gottleib Wogel, gives the following troubled picture:

The masturbator gradually loses his moral faculties; he acquires a dull, silly, listless, embarrassed, sad, effeminate exterior. He becomes indolent; averse to and incapable of all intellectual exertion; all presence of mind deserts him; his feeble soul succumbs to the lightest task; his memory daily losing more and more, he is unable to comprehend the most common things, or to connect the simplest

185

ideas; previously acquired knowledge is forgotten; all the vivacity, all the pride, all the qualities of the spirit by which these unfortunates formerly subjugated or attracted their equals, abandon them, and leave them no longer aught but contempt.

The last crisis of melancholy and the most frightful suggestions of despair commonly end in hastening the death of these unfortunates, or else they fall into complete apathy, and sunken below those brutes which have the least instinct, they retain only the figure of their race.

[A Physician, *Satan.*]

A MAN WHO HAS BEEN DEEPLY IN LOVE WITH HIMSELF SHOULDN'T RUSH INTO MARRIAGE

Should a Young Man Marry After Self-abuse for Years?—It is always best for a young man who has practiced this vice for three, five, or ten years to cease the habit for a year or two before marrying.

But, if he has indulged only in a very limited way, postponement of marriage is not necessary.

[Shannon, *Personal Help*, p. 274.]

SELF-ABUSE IS NOT ALWAYS INCURABLE: HOW ONE VICTIM WAS SUCCESSFULLY TREATED

In our immediate neighborhood lived an intelligent, good and sensible couple. They had a boy about five years of age who was growing fretful, pale and puny. After trying all other remedies to restore him to vigor of body and mind, they journeyed from place to place, hoping to leave the offending cause behind.

186

I had often suggested to the mother that "self-abuse" might be the cause, but no, she would not have it so, and said, "You must be mistaken, as he has inherited no such tendencies, nor has he been taught it by playmates—we have guarded him carefully."

Finally, however, she took up a medical book and made a study of it and, after much thought, said, "I cannot believe it, yet it describes Charlie's case exactly. I will watch."

To her surprise, she found, notwithstanding all her convictions to the contrary, that Charlie was a victim to this loathsome habit.

On going to his bed, after he had gone to sleep, she found his hands still upon the organ, just as they were when he fell asleep. She watched this carefully for a few days, then took him in her confidence and told him of the dreadful evil effects. Finding the habit so firmly fixed, she feared that telling him, at this age, what effect it would have upon his future would not eradicate the evil as soon as she hoped, so, after studying the case for a time, she hit upon the following remedy. Although unscientific, literally speaking, it had the desired effect. Feeling that something must be done to stop, and stop at once, the awful habit, she said, "Did you know, Charlie, that if you keep up this habit of 'self-abuse' that a brown spot will come on your abdomen, light brown at first, and grow darker each week, until it eats a sore right into your system, and if it keeps on, will eventually kill you?"

After Charlie had gone to sleep, and finding his hands again on the sexual organs, to prove to him the truth of her argument, she took a bottle of "Iodine" and, with the cork, put on the abdomen a quantity sufficient to give it a light-brown color, and about the size of a pea. Next night, in bathing him, she discovered the spot, and said, "Look! Already it has come!"

The boy cried out in very fear, and promised not to repeat it again.

The next night the mother put on a second application which made the spot still darker and a trifle sore. Charlie watched the spot as he would a reptile that was lurking about to do his deadly work—and the mother was never again obliged to use the "Iodine."

[Melendy, *Perfect Womanhood.*]

The NEW WAY

The OLD WAY

188

ATTENTION, MOTHERS: HEED THIS MESSAGE AND SAVE YOUR SON'S LIFE!

I say to you, mother, and oh, so earnestly: "Go teach your boy that which you may never be ashamed to do, about those organs that make him specially a boy."

Teach him they are called sexual organs, that they are not impure, but of special importance, and made by God for a definite purpose.

If he has ever learned to handle his sexual organs, or to touch them in any way except to keep them clean, tell him not to do it again. If he does, he will not grow up happy, healthy and strong.

Teach him that when he handles or excites the sexual organs, all parts of the body suffer, because they are connected by nerves that run throughout the system, this is why it is called "self-abuse." The whole body is abused when this part of the body is handled or excited in any manner whatever.

Teach them to shun all children who indulge in this loathsome habit or all children who talk about these things. The sin is terrible, and is, in fact, worse than lying or stealing! For, although these are wicked and will ruin their soul, yet this habit of self-abuse will ruin both soul and body.

If the sexual organs are handled, it brings too much blood to these parts, and produces a diseased condition; it also causes disease in other organs of the body because they are left with a less amount of blood than they ought to have. The sexual organs, too, are very closely connected with the spine and the brain by means of the nerves, and if they are handled, or if you keep thinking about them, these nerves get excited and become exhausted, and this makes the back ache, the brain heavy and the whole body weak.

It lays the foundation for consumption, paralysis and heart disease, it weakens the memory, makes a boy careless, negligent and listless.

It even makes many lose their minds; others, when grown, commit suicide.

How often mothers see their little boys handling themselves, and let it pass, because they think the boy will outgrow the habit, and do not realize the strong hold it has upon them! l say to you who love your boys — "Watch!"

189

Don't think that it does no harm to your boy because he does not suffer now, for the effects of this vice come on so slowly that the victim is often very near death before you realize that he has done himself harm.

[Melendy, *Perfect Womanhood.*]

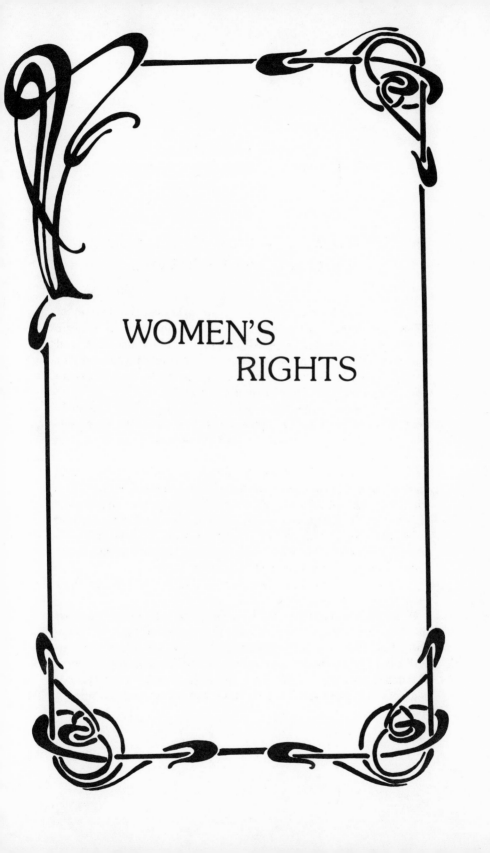

WOMEN'S RIGHTS

THE SUREST WAY TO DEBASE A WOMAN IS TO ALLOW HER TO VOTE˙

If carried out in actual practice, this matter of "Women's Rights" will speedily eventuate in the most prolific source of her wrongs. She will become rapidly unsexed, and degraded from her present exalted position to the level of man, without his advantages; she will cease to be the gentle mother, and become the Amazonian brawler.

The chivalric veneration with which man now regards woman arises from the distance, as well as the difference, between them; in fact, from the advantages she possesses as woman.

This would vanish with her political equality, for he would then be in perpetual and open strife and rivalry against her; whether as a political enemy or political ally, the distinctions of sex will be forgotten, and she will lose that respect and deference with which she has hitherto been so generously endowed; she will be treated rather as man than as woman; "she cannot have the advantages of both sexes at once."

Nature, not legislators, has assigned to the two sexes their respective spheres.

Observe the families of those women who devote almost their entire time and attention to even meritorious and essentially feminine, but outside works—how neglected and proverbially wild and ungovernable are the children. Everyone says of such a woman, "She does good in a general way, but neglects her poor family, who have the prior claim to her attention."

192

WOMAN'S TRADITIONAL PLACE

But how is it with those women who neglect these sacred duties to follow schemes of ambition or of pleasure?

They are justly regarded as monstrosities.

Extend the suffrage to woman, throw her into the political arena, set her squabbling and scheming for office, and you multiply indefinitely the number of monstrosities.

Indeed, with female suffrage "political intrigue" will gain a new and even worse significance than it now enjoys. It will certainly prove an additional and very powerful danger for woman's chastity.

[A Physician, *Satan.*]

WOMEN'S RIGHTS: A DANGEROUS EPIDEMIC

The latest modern invention, which we fear will plague the inventors, is the proposition that women are entitled to the same "privileges" as men in conducting political affairs, and in all offices of honor and emolument now monopolized by the "sterner sex."

This heresy has been christened by the seductive cognomen of "Women's Rights."

Set in motion by a singular class of advocates, it would almost seem to have become epidemic.

As though dissatisfied with irksome lullaby and the wearisome routine of household duties, hosts have joined the invading forces, and now their conventions, their speeches, their special organs, and their sophisticated catch-words have assumed so great proportions that they really seem on the verge of securing political prominence.

The fierce and indomitable energy of the American people, which has survived the most mighty social and political revolution of this world, must and will have some fiery excitement with which to occupy itself; and, having just ridden down its pet hobbyhorse of slavery, it has seized upon this bauble of Women's Rights, and bids fair to dignify it into a terrible engine of destruction.

Let us examine what it will do for our daughters in its present aspect, and what if carried to successful operation.

The mere discussion of such a revolution as a possibility, the bare toleration of the idea, is sufficient in itself to injure the mind to operate powerfully upon the imagination of these impressionable creatures — to excite in them feelings of indignation and dissatisfaction with their present condition.

Every argument that ingenuity can suggest, is brought to bear in assuring them that they are deprived of certain inherent "rights" by an unjust and tyrannical age. It is but of little moment to them what these so-called rights may be; the feeling that they exist and that they are unjustly withheld is sufficient to occasion a sort of sentimental rebellion dangerous to tranquil repose and to feminine modesty.

[A Physician, *Satan.*]

IT IS WELL-KNOWN THAT ALL MEN ARE
INHERENTLY MORE INTELLIGENT
THAN ALL WOMEN, BUT . . .

There is now and then a woman who, in constitution and proclivities, may be considered as an exception to the rule.

Strongly constituted, endowed with intellectual qualities superior to her sex, with broad and high forehead like a man, she is a sort of mistake of Nature.

Such women are generally wanting in the qualities which inspire the love of man, and so, as in the harmony of things force must be united to weakness, these masculine women nearly always ally themselves with blanched males, weak physically and mentally, capable of receiving the authority which their wives' needs must exercise. The parts are simply reversed, that is all, but the phenomenon is not pleasant.

Nearly every prominent advocate of Women's Rights now before the public, is of this class, and, if married, she is thus coupled.

If it were consistent with politeness we could specify these coincidences, *ad nauseam*.

[A Physician, *Satan.*]

IF WOMEN'S-RIGHTS VIRAGOES HAD THEIR
WAY, GIRLS WOULD BE SHAVING

Making Women Masculine — Nothing proves so irrefutably the hopelessness of the task undertaken by a few' "strong- minded" women — namely, to equalize the sexes by making women more masculine — than the fact thus revealed by anthropology and history: that the tendency of civilization has been to make men and women more and more unlike, physically and emotionally.

What ever approximation there may have been has been en-

195

tirely on the part of the men, who have become less coarse or "manly," in the old acceptation of that term, and more femininely refined; while women have endeavored to maintain the old distance by a corresponding increase of refinement on their part.

Should the Women's Rights viragoes ever succeed in establishing their social ideal, when women will share all the men's privileges, make stump speeches, and—of course—go back to the harvest fields and to war with them—then goodbye, Romantic Love!

But there is no danger that these Amazons will ever carry their point. They might as well try to convince women to wear beards; or men, crinolines.

[Finck, *Romantic Loves*, pp. 175-76.]

GIRLS ON PARADE.

WOMEN'S RIGHTS; OR, WHY ONLY LAYING HENS HAVE THE RIGHT TO CACKLE

This Women's Rights Movement All Wrong—Both the entire spirit and manner of this whole reform, falsely so called, deserve severe censure.

It starts with a wrong object, which it prosecutes in a way most objectionable and calculated to thwart the very ends sought. Its modus operandi is quite like one man clubbing another with "Give me my rights, I tell you!" and instantly repeating the blow with, "Then give me my rights this instant, you old heathen!"

It is conducted chiefly by dissatisfied wives, or else by unmarried croakers, most of whom are in a grumbling mood.

The very look and entire aspect of these "strong-minded women too plainly declare that their affections have been reversed, and that disappointed love has thoroughly soured them throughout. What one of them all is in a warm, gushing, genial, plastic affectionate mood? Only those who have any "right" to say one word; yet those have no word to say. Waiting for such to move in these rights' movements would be like waiting for the water to stop running.

At least, unmarried novices, though forty, are improper spokesmen. Only laying hens have any right to cackle.

Let those speak who know something by experience—that best of teachers. This entire movement is directly calculated to breed conjugal disaffection.

Effeminate men naturally take and propose to these strongly masculinized women, yet most vigorous human males "pass by" such women "on the other side"; because these commanding, independent, authoritative, positive women, who insist on overruling family affairs, must either marry tame weak-minded, putty men, who are two thirds women, and therefore willing to serve under them, or else create a conflict of jurisdiction.

There are a few just such tame automaton machines, just adapted to these arbitrary, driving, two thirds masculine strong-minded "woman's rights" wives, who love to command, conduct business, lead off, and take the responsibility; while these easy, lazy shiftless, inert husbands will endure to be henpecked.

This is a wise adaption for both, because such men without such women would starve; and such women, with positive men, would foment strife perpetually.

[Fowler, *Sexual Science*, pp. 141-43.]

UNLESS WOMEN PRACTICE MORE AMERICANISM, OUR NATION IS DOOMED

Americanism — By this term I designate an unhealthy feature of sexual life, common among the educated classes of the United States, and apparently originating in the greed for dollars, which is more prevalant in North America than anywhere else.

I refer to the unnatural life which Americans lead, and more especially to its sexual aspect.

American women consider muscular work and labor in the country as degrading to their sex. This is a relic of the days of slavery when all manual labor was left to Negroes, and is so to a great extent today.

Desirous of remaining young and fresh as long as possible, fearing the dangers and troubles of childbirth and the bringing- up of children, the American woman has an increasing aversion to pregnancy, childbirth, suckling and the rearing of large families.

It is evident that this form of emancipation of women is absolutely deleterious and that it leads to a degeneration, if not to extinction of the race.

The mixed Aryan (European) race of North America will diminish and become gradually extinguished, even without emigration, and will soon be replaced by Chinese or Negroes.

It is necessary for woman to labor as well as man, and she ought not avoid the fulfillment of her natural position.

Every race which does not understand this necessity ends in extinction.

198

MOTHER—THE MOST SACRED WORD IN THE ENGLISH LANGUAGE.

A woman's ideal ought not to consist in reading novels and lolling in rocking chairs, nor in working only in offices and shops, so as to preserve her delicate skin and graceful figure.

She ought to develop herself strongly and healthily by working along with man in body and mind, and by procreating numerous children, when she is strong, robust and intelligent.

[Forel, *Sexual Question,* pp. 331-32.]

SUCCESSFUL
PARENTHOOD

WHY THE LITTLE TYKE OFTEN LOOKS JUST LIKE THE BUTCHER, THE BAKER, AND THE CANDLESTICK MAKER

No man should ever beget a child without weeks, perhaps months, of preparation for this important office.

He should live temperately, soberly, chastely. If he has bad habits, he should, during this period at least, carefully abstain from indulging them. He should cultivate purity of thought, and seek thorough and intelligent sympathy with his wife in all her hopes and aims.

The importance of the moment of conception is not generally understood. Goethe aptly illustrates this in his "Elective Affinities."

A husband and wife, each loving another, and each thinking of that other at the instant of sexual intercourse, found evidence of their mutual unfaithfulness when the child was born, for it presented in its face the double likeness of the lovers whom the parents had in mind.

[Lewis, *Chastity*, p. 158.]

202

SPARE THE WHIP, SAVE THE CHILD

That passion may be induced, however, by castigation or whipping is so well established that parents and nurses would do well to avoid the practice generally.

[Parke, *Sexuality.*]

IT'S EASY TO CHOOSE THE SEX OF YOUR CHILD. JUST FOLLOW THESE SIMPLE DIRECTIONS

When a Male Child Is Desired — The husband should partake of good substantial food. Exercise in open air; indulge in light literature; keep up a glow of spirits; abstain from indulgence for a short time previous to the procreative period. During this period, the wife should abstain from animal foods, living mostly on vegetables and farinaceous articles of diet, exercise daily almost to fatigue and pass a portion of her time with females older than herself.

When a Female Child Is Desired — Exactly the opposite course should be pursued — the woman should indulge in the most stimulating food — but should not indulge her passions, reserving her whole vigor for the desired time. The male should indulge in violent physical exercise to fatigue, and morning and night take sitz baths of cold rock-salt water.

SHE MUST HAVE BEEN A BEAUTIFUL BABY— HER MOTHER WENT TO MUSEUMS

During the early stages of pregnancy, as well as at all subsequent periods, it is desirable that the mother have at

203

hand, for frequent contemplation, some of the best works of art, in statuary, or pictures, or both, as models of the beautiful and graceful in form, and of the amiable and noble in expression. Perhaps some one admired figure may be chosen, to be copied by the mother's wonderful electrotyping power in her living work of art; but care should be taken that it be one in which goodness as well as physical beauty is bodied forth.

In this is to be found one of the' noblest uses of art; and there can be no doubt that the works of the great masters have had more effect than the world imagines in producing and multiplying forms of beauty and manliness through impressions made on the minds of matrons.

[Melendy, *Perfect Womanhood.*]

YOU, TOO, CAN BE THE PROUD PARENT OF A ROCKEFELLER, FORD OR EDISON

That a mother may, during the period of gestation, exercise great influence, by her own mental and physical action, either unwittingly or purposely in such a way as to determine the traits and tendencies of her offspring, is now a common belief among all intelligent people.

The assertion has been made that "it is for the mother, by the use of appropriate means to produce a poet, a thinker, an artist, an inventor, a philanthropist, or any other type of manhood or womanhood, desirable or undesirable, as she will."

An author, Dr. Brittan, who has given much study to the occult problems of human life, gives the following facts: "A woman, who, during the period of gestation, was chiefly employed in reading the poets and in giving form to her daydreams of the ideal world, at the same time may give to her child large, ideality, and a highly imaginative turn of mind."

Some time since we met with a youth who has finely molded limbs and a symmetrical form throughout. His mother has a large lean attenuated frame, that does not offer so much as a single suggestion of the beautiful. The boy is doubtless indebted for his fine form to the presence of a beautiful French lithograph in his mother's sleeping apartment, and which presented for her contemplation the faultless form of a naked child.

[Melendy, *Perfect Womanhood.*]

TOILET TRAINING IS IMPORTANT, BUT
MORAL TRAINING SHOULD COME FIRST

Every mother has an ideal career for her offspring, and as the tastes and capacity of the child develop if they indicate capacity in the desired direction, encouragement and aid in the way, perhaps, of toys, pictures and books are afforded; if the childish inclinations seem contrary to the hopes and wishes of the parents, counteracting influences are brought into requisition.

This is the beginning of what is termed excellent training or "bringing up" and it may be followed with necessary modifications until the child attain to maturity, and yet the man or woman becomes a libertine or an outcast. The mother dies of a broken heart, feeling, perhaps, that Providence is unjust and unkind in its dealing with her, but not once questioning the fact that her whole duty has been done.

Under precisely the conditions I have mentioned I heard a mother complain of God and justify herself, saying, "I began his moral training when he was a baby, and as soon as he could walk and talk he was taught to pray."

She could not realize that she had begun too late the process of mind and morals building.

That mothers-to-be should dwell in an atmosphere of tenderness and love has long been conceded; but the prevalent idea that they should be indulged and thus encouraged in outbursts of temper, fits of jealousy, envy, covetousness, and other undesirable qualities which often assert themselves to an unusual degree under such conditions, is wrong. This is the time

The Two Paths

What Will the Girl Become?

AT 13
BAD LITERATURE

AT 13
STUDY & OBEDIENCE

AT 20
FLIRTING & COQUETTERY

AT 20
VIRTUE & DEVOTION

AT 26
FAST LIFE & DISSIPATION

AT 26
A LOVING MOTHER

AT 40
AN OUTCAST

AT 60
AN HONORED GRANDMOTHER

206

The Two Paths

AT 15
STUDY & CLEANLINESS

AT 25
PURITY & ECONOMY

AT 36
HONORABLE SUCCESS

AT 60
VENERABLE OLD AGE

What Will The Boy Become?

AT 15
CIGARETTES & SELF-ABUSE

AT 25
IMPURITY & DISSIPATION

AT 36
VICE & DEGENERACY

AT 48
MORAL-PHYSICAL WRECK

207

of all times when such sentiments should be overcome. I have no doubt that the greater number of the world's professional thieves might truthfully assign their evil propensity to abnormal covetousness on the part of their mother before their birth, rather than to thieving ancestors!

I believe, too, that were it possible to trace the worse cases of hopeless insanity to first causes they would be found in ungoverned rather than ungovernable temper in the mother.

There is no limit to the evil a mother may entail upon her unborn child; while on the other hand it is impossible to picture the happy results her efforts may accomplish.

[Melendy, *Perfect Womanhood.*]

IF YOUR BABY IS A CHIP OFF YOUR FIRST HUSBAND'S BLOCK, THERE MAY BE AN ACCEPTABLE EXPLANATION

Another point worthy of mention here is the well-known fact that the intimate association of married people modifies even the physical form of both. Almost everyone has noticed how much alike in appearance married people often come to be who have lived many years together. This physical change undoubtedly extends farther than to the features only. The whole constitution is modified.

A remarkable illustration is found in the frequent observation that children of a woman by a second husband often resemble in appearance the first husband much more than their own father.

It has been observed that the children of Negro women, even by husbands of pure Negro blood, are much lighter in color than usual, if she has had a child by a white man previously.

[Kellog, *Plain Facts.*]

208

SURE, "MY SON THE ACCOUNTANT" SOUNDS ATTRACTIVE, BUT HE MAY BE MUCH BETTER OFF AS A SHEPHERD

If a youth is delicate it is a common practice among parents either to put him to some light indoor trade, or if it can be afforded, to one of the learned professions. Such a practice is absurd and full of danger.

The close confinement of an indoor trade is highly prejudicial to health. The hard reading requisite to fit a man to fill, for instance, the sacred office, only increases any delicacy of constitution. The stooping at a desk, in an attorney's office, is most trying to the chest. The harass, *(sic)*, anxiety, disturbed nights, interrupted meals, and intense study necessary to fit a man for the medical profession is still more dangerous to health than either law, divinity, or any indoor trade.

If a boy is delicate or of consumptive habit, an outdoor calling should be advised, such as that of a farmer, a tanner, a land surveyor or a butcher. Tanners and butchers are seldom known to die of consumption.

I cannot refrain from reprobating the too common practice among parents of bringing up their boys to the professions. The anxieties and the heartaches which they undergo if they do not succeed materially injure the health.

[Melendy, *Perfect Womanhood.*]

A FINAL WORD

A PERSONAL NOTE TO THE
SEXUALLY TROUBLED

The author of this work is often applied to personally or by letter for advice, by both young women and young men desiring to marry or contemplating marriage.

One thinks he or she has some physical malformation, injury or infirmity which would render such a step unadvisable. Another fears the law of mental and physical adaption will be disregarded, followed with conjugal unhappiness, if a certain pending courtship should result in marriage, or an actual engagement be fulfilled, and daguerreotypes or photographs of both parties, with descriptions of persons and characters, are presented for my decision and advice.

Other matters of similar import are frequently laid before me in personal consultations or by letter.

As these matters require time, and often considerable consideration, and do not belong to the ordinary labors of a physician, a fee of $5 will be charged for all such advice.

Advice of this character will, at all times, be cheerfully given, if these terms are complied with, and all such consultations will be treated with entire confidence.

[Edward B. Foote, M.D. (author of "Medical Common Sense"; "Improvement of Marriage"; and "Causes of Insanity"), *Dr. Foote's New Plain Home Talk on Love, Marriage, and Parentage* — A Fair and Earnest Discussion of Human, Social and Marital Relations in All Ages and Countries; Defects in Marriage Systems and Remedies; Human Temperaments and Adaptation; Based on Studies in Sexual Psychology (New York: Murray Hill, 1901), p. 1197.]

INDEX

211

212